THE
MILLENNIAL
MOVEMENT

Surviving The Corporate Transition

A Simple Guide for Professional Success

Rashida Selise Wilson

Contributing Author-Tayna Frett

IN DUE SEASON
Publishing

The Millennial Movement
Surviving The Corporate Transition

For more information contact: www.selisespeakslife.com
selisespeakslife@yahoo.com

Typesetting, Book Layout, Editing and Cover Design by
Enger Lanier Taylor for In Due Season Publishing

Photography and Makeup: Toya Poplar for Tree of Life Photography

Published By: In Due Season Publishing
Huntsville, Alabama
indueseasonpublishing@gmail.com

ISBN-13: 978-0972745659
ISBN-10: 0972745653

Disclaimer:

This book contains information that is intended only to educate and inform. This information is a matter of the author's experience and opinion. The publisher and author do not offer any legal or other professional counsel. In the case of a need for any such expertise, consult with the appropriate professional. The author and publisher shall have no liability or responsibility to any person or entity regarding any loss or damage incurred, or alleged to have incurred, directly or indirectly, by the information contained in this book. This book does not contain all information available on the subject matter. This book has not been created to be specific to any individual's or organization's situation or need.

Contents

Thank You

I am so grateful for the opportunity to finally motivate, inspire and empower people to live life on purpose! I know that it is part of my Kingdom assignment and I certainly could not do it alone. I want to say *thank you* to those who have helped me along this journey and throughout the process of completing this project. I want to especially thank every new and aspiring professional for giving me permission to impart into your life.

Blessings to you!
Rashida

Special Thanks To

My Lord and Savior Jesus Christ, for gracing me for this assignment. I am honored to be used for global impact.

My hubby (Edward Wilson) - Your love, support and consistency exemplifying God's love is priceless. I thank and love you!

My babies (Ezkeiel and India) – I press because of you. There is no greateer love.

My mom and dad (Teresa and Wellington Brown Sr.) You are the best parents a girl could ever have. I love you dearly!

My contributing author and BFF#1 (Tayna and brother (not in-law) Marsh - The value you add to my life is amazing. You two have always been my greatest supporters!

My baby sis, BFF#2 and favorite entrepreneur (Christina) – You inspire me to change the world! I love you!

My baby brother and mini dad (Wellington Brown Jr.) - I love you and your heart! You encourage me to pray and believe!

In Due Season Publishing - for your relentless effort to complete my first project.

My Professional Journey

"No matter what we have failed to accomplish, we have accomplished something without failure"- Rashida

If I told you that my professional journey was easy, I would be telling you an untruth. However, if I told you that it was worth every lesson learned, I would be honestly preparing you for what to expect during this next phase in your life. While everyone's journey may be unique, one thing is guaranteed; all roads will lead to professional growth and eventually success if you are committed and coachable.

When most 11 year olds were spending their summers at the poolside or sitting on the front steps listening to music, playing hopscotch and running behind ice cream trucks, I remember sitting in my basement in Queens, New York either lining up my baby dolls, handing out test scores, registering them for school, or you would find me standing in front of a mirror with a brush in my hand pretending to be holding a microphone. I would practice answering questions or interviewing others without stumbling over my words. Surprisingly, I had no idea that I would be a teacher, presenter, trainer, motivational speaker, radio host or anything of the sort.

It is funny how full-circle life moments happen. Now do not get me wrong, I had fun as a kid, but it was a balance of fun and future preparation. I can remember my very first job as if it were yesterday. I worked at my aunt's store in Brooklyn, New York greeting and assisting customers and checking them out at the register. I was exposed to entrepreneurship and taught the value of hard work at a very early age. One year later at the age of 12, I started a volunteer job at a local hospital as a candy striper. My parents actually paid me a weekly wage to encourage me and teach me responsibility.

By the time I turned 14, I was offered a part-time position working in a law firm 3-4 days per week after school. During the summers, I worked full-time. I worked there until I graduated. I learned everything from how to work the law library, to assisting in the accounting, billing and other departments. Finally, I worked extensively in Human Resources, which was actually my first exposure to that occupation. By the time I was 18 and ready to graduate high school, I had been fully introduced to the corporate arena. This included everything from office etiquette, to understanding how to identify and navigate around office politics. I worked at several law firms as well as several retail jobs and other corporate environments for a number of years.

I wanted to go away to college. However, my parents were completely opposed and convinced that I would not be successful that far away from home. I then decided that I was not ready to attend college at all. So, I waited a few years and kept working. I was blessed to land a number of great jobs that groomed me for my career. I was eventually offered an opportunity as a front office manager in a pretty nice company which quickly resulted in promotion to office manager. This was my first permanent job with benefits and growth potential.

I was excited! I always prided myself in having a solid work ethic, which always seemed to result in promotion opportunities.

I learned the company and eventually took on several other major responsibilities that included HR and managing an office team staff of 5. It was great experience to have my first supervisor and management role at the age of 23. I had to do everything from hiring and training, to disciplinary actions, performance reviews and unfortunately even terminations. I can recall my boss, the owner at the time, taking me under his wing and teaching me all about the corporate arena. I was honored to have this astute businessman take an interest in helping me to grow. I was the office manager for four years while I attended college at night. The company eventually decided to go public and was sold. When they went public, there were several layoffs and my position was one of them. I was sad to be losing my first solid job where I had grown so much professionally and personally. I hated to see the season change, but I realized that it was all a part of a much bigger picture and it definitely helped me to start my career with a solid foundation.

I had just graduated with my Bachelor's degree and received a nice severance package, so I took that opportunity to leave New York and try something new. With my degree in hand and several years of experience and training under my belt, I was officially a professional and ready for a change. I eventually moved to Huntsville, Alabama to relax and enjoy my summer with family. By the fall, I was working again as the marketing office manager for a brand new, $52 million dollar continuing care retirement community during their pre-opening phase. Approximately six months later, I was asked what I would be interested in doing once the community officially opened. I had no idea because I had no clinical experience, therefore, nursing positions were not an option and I did not really have enough human resource experience to justify being the HR Manager in a facility of that magnitude. However, I requested that I be considered for the HR Manager position; long story short, I GOT THE POSITION! I was finishing up my Master's of Science in Management degree just in time for the Grand Opening and was officially hired as the new HR Manager for this amazing community. I was humbled and blessed by this opportunity. This was my introduction to the healthcare industry and I loved it.

As you can see, I am no stranger to hard work, so I was willing to do whatever it took to prove that they made the right decision. I worked some nights until 2 or 3 in the morning preparing to hire new employees and conducting job fairs and trainings for hundreds of potential staff. I was committed to teamwork and whatever it took to be successful. I worked that position for several years and left to work for another prominent healthcare company as the HR and Recruitment Director for a few years. I transitioned from Huntsville to Maryland for a few years and it was not long before I was offered an HR Manager position at a manufacturing association, where I learned more about serving my director and the benefits of being coachable. I also had the privilege of participating in hiring a number of employees, which included upper-level positions such as VPs and CEOs.

During this time in my career, I also hired several new college graduates, which we referred to as junior professionals. The experience with that population is what actually prompted my desire to write this book. I did recruitment work for several years. After which, I started my part-time consulting business. trained and coached clients for professional success, while I continued to work in the corporate world. I must say that during my 20 year career in HR and administration, I have had the opportunity of working for and serving under the mentorship of some very wealthy, wise and astute professionals and business owners who have taken the time to correct me, coach me and guide me along my personal and professional journey.

I have learned some tough lessons along the way that groomed and prepared me at every stage of my professional transition. Whether it was a promotion within the same organization or growth outside of the organization, I was prepared for the next open door every time. However, the growth and advancement did not come without its challenges.

As mentioned, I have seen and experienced quite a bit as it relates to hiring individuals on all levels. As much as I loved the recruitment and hiring process and even more so the excitement of calling the final chosen candidate and offering them an opportunity to join the company, nothing disheartened me more than young, energetic and educated professionals who could have been offered a great entry level position, but missed out because they were either not trained on how to brand, market and sell themselves or how to properly position themselves for success once hires.

During my career, I have witnessed both the success of smart young professionals who have gleaned from the wisdom and experience of seasoned professionals that were at their disposal, positioning themselves for amazing success. I have also witnessed many imprudent young professionals who chose not to leverage the knowledge, wisdom and experience at their disposal. Instead they had an entitlement mentality only to find themselves tripping up the corporate ladder looking for the corner office, the next promotion and monetary gain, finding nothing but a revolving door of frustration and disappointment.

After years of watching and speaking with young professionals who really wanted to be successful, but needed guidance, I decided to help by sharing my experiences. I am a firm believer that when opportunities present themselves, everyone should have a fair chance at the opportunity. Unfortunately, many young professionals are not equipped with the tools and insight on how to survive the corporate transition.

I have learned, in order to achieve success in your career endeavors, you must understand two very important keys. First, you must learn how to transition into the corporate arena with humility. Second, you must know how to grow in the corporate arena with wisdom and integrity. You can always learn technical job related skills in the classroom, but you can only learn the simple and easily applicable truths shared in this book through experience or observation.

This simple resource has been written to help you avoid some common professional pitfalls. I will honestly share what 20 years of corporate grooming has taught me. My hope is that the practical advice and nuggets shared in this resource will position you for professional success as you embark upon your journey. NOW Pursue!

Chapter 1

Package YOU!
Pursuing The Opportunity

"We should not let our fears hold us back from pursuing our hopes"
John Fitzgerald Kennedy

In the words of Benjamin Franklin, "If you fail to plan, you plan to fail." This statement couldn't be more accurate when it comes to executing a successful job search. When you decide it is time to begin the search, it is imperative that you prepare and plan, plan, plan and plan some more. Organizing yourself and resources so that you can maximize your search time and remain on task is very important. The career search can be fun and exciting at first, but can quickly become daunting and frustrating when you find yourself sending out countless resumes, making phone calls and patiently waiting, but not hearing back.

The truth is every job seeker experiences this, but the uphill battle is much easier to conquer when you have resources in place. The most important part of the process begins with a tenacious mindset and choosing to be committed to the journey. You must be determined to succeed even when it gets discouraging. I can recall my own job search process being tiring and discouraging many days. I was determined to successfully find a decent job. I also talked to a few pretty successful professional colleagues and asked them about their experience when they were unemployed. "How did you eventually get the job you had been looking for?" I asked. The response I received was consistent with everyone I met. They all stated that they treated the job search like a job itself. They approached each day as if they were going to work and diligently "pounded the pavement", which included, going to job fairs, placement agencies, and all types of networking functions, until they saw some fruit from their labor.

Whether it was online searches and completing applications, to spending time at the library mapping out a plan, every day was treated like a dedicated hard day at work until each person started receiving the results they wanted. There is no secret or way around it. This process will require commitment and dedication, but it is quite rewarding when the calls start rolling in. However, you must decide to be successful at any and all cost. It will be worth it. During this process, prepare to deal with distractions and even personal feelings of inadequacy and self-defeating talk. Nevertheless, you need to keep pushing.

Some days you will be your best cheerleader, but at other times your own worst critic by doubting yourself. Especially when the adrenaline of everything leading up to graduation day wears off and weeks have passed and still no job yet. I'm not trying to be a "Debbie Downer," I just want to be realistic about the emotions you can anticipate so you are not caught off guard. I promise, if you plan and give it some time, your dedication and hard work will pay off.

I remember hearing a story of a little girl standing at the top of a staircase screaming at the top of her lungs, "Let Me GO!" Later she realized that she was standing on her own pant leg. I caution you not to get in your own way. Set realistic goals and carve out time to focus and work. Chart your course and stay positive. You can do it, but it will require a plan and dedication.

You will also need a few tangible resources, including a reliable computer and internet access for job searches and resume revisions. The library is always an available resource. However, I love internet cafes and coffee shops because they offer a nice ambiance, as well as free internet. You will also need to create a professional and mature email address specifically for job searches. Another helpful tool is a job search tracking sheet, which can be created in Excel to include columns like company name, date, position applied for, date and time of follow-up call, name of contact, if you spoke with someone, and finally a column for next steps. This sheet will help you keep on top of your outreach efforts. Finally you need to be sure to have a working telephone number with a professional voicemail or just a generic message. In addition to your cell phone number, a Google voice number is free and always a good back-up in the event your cell phone number gives you problems. These are just a few helpful tools to make your search process seamless and successful.

The very next thing that every young professional pursuing an opportunity will need is the right attitude and a positive professional outlook. Remember, no one owes you anything. Whatever you want, you need to work hard to receive. A positive attitude and professional perspective spells success, even if you do not obtain the first opportunity you pursue. A positive attitude helps you to keep moving forward despite rejection. Truthfully, it may take a little time to get a job and maybe even more time to get into your career field. So, not only must you have a positive attitude about yourself, but it's equally important to have a positive attitude about what you have to offer when it is time to meet a potential employer.

Many young professionals typically have some intern experience prior to graduating. However, if you do not, or what you have is not substantial, it is ok! Experience will come over time. Just remember you always have something to offer, even if this is your first potential job opportunity. Remember, your volunteer experience in any capacity is very valuable. Whether you have been the captain on a sports team at school, head of a debate club, a part of the student body leadership or a babysitting job after school, you always have something to offer. You just need to take time to figure out what it is.

I have also learned during my career as an HR professional, and I am sure other employers will agree, the most valuable asset you can offer that cannot be learned in a classroom, or from a book, is how to be pleasant, peaceful, positive and personable. The value those soft skills bring to the table is priceless. Remember, you are gifted and skilled well before you gain any concrete work experience. You must see yourself as valuable before you begin the process and it will make all of the difference in how you approach the process. Confidence sells. If you need confidence boosting, identify a mentor or coach to help you during this process.

> *How you see yourself will determine how you sell yourself.*

It is also very important to learn as much as you can about the current job market when planning and preparing your career search. To stay ahead of the game you must be knowledgeable and marketable. The more informed you are, the higher your chances are for success. Things change so frequently that it would be in your best interest to stay abreast of the corporate climate at all times. Find out what careers and industries are hot and which ones are becoming obsolete.

With technology, so many careers that were valued years ago are now being replaced or even outsourced. Do some research on current salaries being offered and what your career field will look like in 10 years to make educated decisions on your career path. You never want to overshoot, but you certainly never want to lowball yourself, underestimating your value and worth. Career coaches can help you with this process so that you can successfully identify the opportunity that is a good combination of your education, skills and passion and earn a decent salary as well. Regardless of your path, do your research.

I am a firm believer that the best decisions are made with the most information. There is nothing more impressive than interviewing an educated young professional who understands the industry, current economic climate and if asked is able to intelligently and realistically discuss the industry, the career opportunity, benefits, salary and more.

It is no secret that the job market has become more strained over the years with the instability of the economy. However, despite economic instability, companies are still hiring and there are many existing career opportunities. So why are qualified candidates not securing positions? There is no logical answer other than the notion that job seekers are uninformed about what it takes to successfully connect a prepared and properly packaged product (you) to an outstanding opportunity.

The most successful people during these times are those who are resourceful enough to stay abreast of industry trends and relentless enough to continue the process despite rejection. They will seek out career coaching and professional development support as needed. They are also creative enough to identify the hidden job market and wise enough to professionally package and position themselves to soar above the average candidate.

In a nutshell, you must be willing to do whatever it takes to get you through your entire search process and selected. So, plan, focus and prepare to succeed! Finally, when you become weary, you must be able to see light at the end of the tunnel. I can assure you the best opportunity for you is on the horizon.

"My greatest mistake in my professional career was underestimating my worth. I failed to adequately research salaries and positions and as a result, was underpaid and overworked for an extended amount of time. I also limited my professional goals solely to my degree and area of study. I would advise any new professional to explore your options and take advantage of career counselors and life coaches that have the talent and ability to cultivate your passion into a purposeful career."

Danelle McClellan –BA, JD

"One major mistake I made as a young professional was accepting salaries that were offered to me without researching the positions and negotiating for what I was really worth. I was intimidated by others who "pretended" to be smarter than me. I would advise you to know your own strengths and your worth and do not expect others to point them out for you."

Teresa Brown – BBA
Director of Administration

Maintaining a Positive Professional Perspective

Maintaining a positive perspective during your job search is easier said than done. However, as mentioned earlier, it is probably the most important part of this process. You will not be successful without a positive viewpoint. It all comes down to you making the choice to remain optimistic in the face of frustration. You can do it! Start with the right attitude and perspective and handle every part of the process professionally. Then you will be ahead of the game.

Remember, how successful you are during this process is not just about what you have accomplished on paper. The ability to convince the potential employer that you are a total package, which includes your technical, as well as your soft skills, is worth its weight in gold. How personable you are will be another draw. This is why a positive attitude from the onset is important. It is attractive and contagious. Employers can sense it from the moment you engage them both over the telephone and in person. Keep the positivity flowing. Employers are looking for more than just whiz kids, although intelligence is important. They are also looking to hire positive, personable, confident and solution-driven leaders who will champion the organizations vision and are willing to be coached and groomed.

You need the aptitude to do the job. However, the truth is, with a job market so highly saturated with jobseekers, your educational accomplishments could be comparable or may even pale in comparison to the competition. Therefore, there must be something from the start of the process to the finish that differentiates you from the bunch. It is a combination of your technical skills, your glowing personality and your positive perspective. Your energy during your interviews is vital. Employers can clearly see what you have accomplished on paper and can only confirm that you are truly able to do the job once you are hired. However, if your unenthusiastic personality will not even get you in the door, you will never be able to prove your ability.

Remember this process can become very daunting and discouraging at times so being surrounded by a positive support system with the right perspective is also crucially important. During your job search, you must connect with motivated, positive, like-minded and inspiring people who are excited about your potential success and genuinely in your corner. I would encourage you to develop what I refer to as an "A" team. This team consists of accountability partners who will honestly keep you focused and on task. These people are there to keep you accountable, cheer you on and be blatantly honest even when you do not want to hear it. This team will help keep you encouraged as they help you see the process through to completion.

Lastly, every job seeker needs to have a "man in the mirror" conversation to honestly determine strengths and weaknesses in order to effectively package, promote and market themselves. I would recommend every professional to periodically do a personal S.W.O.T analysis as you move along in your career. Basically, you identify your strengths, weaknesses, opportunities and threats to determine how to approach your project, which is the job search or career advancement.

I am amazed at the number of people who have

requested my assistance for professional coaching and were totally oblivious about the next steps they should take in their career search or professional pursuits, simply because they were not aware of how to properly assess their current successes and failures in relation to their overall goals and search. I have had job seekers call me adamant about revising their resume because they were getting calls but, no second interviews. After assessing their phone interview skills it was concluded that the resume was not the problem at all. They clearly needed a little coaching on their telephone interview skills.

Assessing yourself and your process helps to better identify where deficiencies may be. After reviewing my client processes, I decided to sum up the entire job search process into four distinct phases. Phase one includes preparing a solid professional product, that develops your resume and personal presentation. Phase two is preparation for phone interview and or screening that identifies what to do and what not to do. Phase three is preparation for an in person interview, second interview or possible group interview, which details interview etiquette, attire, dialogue guidance and closing statements. Finally, phase four closes the deal with the follow-up and thank you to all of the parties you met during the process. The successful completion of all of these phases will undeniably secure you a great opportunity so remember to plan your pursuit and have the proper professional perspective.

Purposeful Preparation and Presentation

Before any consideration is given for a potential opportunity, employers rely solely on what you submit as a representation of yourself in the form of your cover letter and resume. Those items introduce you to the potential employer long before you even get a telephone call. Therefore, your resume and cover letter must be able to clearly outline your experience and what you have to offer. Whenever you are pursuing an opportunity, you must first understand that you are the product and in order to successfully win the attention of potential employers, you must be properly packaged. Both your tool, which is your cover letter and resume, and your personal presentation must be polished, poised and professional.

I have heard many HR professionals comment that a resume has six seconds to make an impression which means it needs to be impressive at-a-glance. Unfortunately, many job seekers have been imprudently encouraged to liberally express themselves at the expense of many missed opportunities. When it comes to the resume, too often it is presented as a subpar product with typos, errors and poorly written content. As for personal appearance, young men often discount how important it is to stand out with a shirt, tie, slacks and be well groomed, clean cut and shaven. For women, we often neglect to consider that cute and trendy is most likely not the best choice of professional wear for an interview. However, this is merely based on industry. Fashion and design industries embrace uniqueness more so than conservative workplace environments. For example, bold hair colors or even natural hair has become quite popular over the past years. It is important to remember that while it is welcomed now more than in times past, it should still be well kept and professional. If your untamed tresses are a distraction when it comes to interviewing for a job, you must determine how that can be temporarily addressed so you do not forfeit an opportunity.

Also, every professional or aspiring professional should have a few staple items which include a dark blue or black suit or black slacks and a pair of well-kept black dress shoes. I always advise women to purchase a pair of simple pearl earrings and a pearl necklace. A clean professional look during interviews is important. The saying, "less is more", includes make-up and cologne. Be conservative and presentable as if you were planning to meet the CEO or President of the company. You never know who may just pop into the interview. Always be ready. While you should not feel prohibited from freely expressing yourself through your own personal style, you must resolve that if the expression of "self" hinders you from getting in the door of potential career opportunities, you must reevaluate what's important. Am I saying you should change yourself? No. What I am simply suggesting is that you learn to adjust. I have seen many young professionals take the "I'm not changing myself for anyone" approach and that is absolutely the wrong attitude to have. You must be willing to make necessary adjustments in life. As you advance professionally you will see that this is not uncommon. Life is about making adjustments along your journey for what is important at the time. Trust me, if the opportunity is worth it, you would be willing to adjust. I have done it and have found that the doors of opportunity were unlimited.

Chapter 2

Sell YOU!
Securing The Opportunity

"I will prepare and someday my chance will come."
Abraham Lincoln

Image IS Everything

I remember when a person's image was merely focused only on how you dressed and presented yourself in person and while that is still very important, technology has shifted that paradigm. It is now equally important, with the advancement of technology and social media, to be mindful of what images or commentary people find when they Twitter, Facebook, Instagram or Google search your name. Your pictures, status updates, posts and comments on others posts, could be used by employers to draw conclusions about you personally and professionally. You must be careful not to inadvertently exploit yourself leaving potential employers questioning whether or not your personal image can pose an issue if hired. My goal is not to discourage you from the liberty of expressing yourself. I am more concerned about you preparing to advance professionally. Therefore, keep in mind that a lot of consideration must be given to how your freedom of expression could potentially hinder your professional advancement. First impressions are usually the final impression.

Contrary to what you might think, you only have one time to make a great first impression. Once you have presented and introduced yourself the first time, you can be sure that however you are perceived at that point is what will be imprinted in the mind of the other person whenever they think of you. You do not get a second chance. How you present yourself in speech, attire, conduct and overall conversation is what you will be judged on. Is that fair? Not always, but it is reality. So get it right the first time. As you present yourself in person, always greet the person who is interviewing you with a firm handshake, a smile and direct eye contact. During your conversations with the interviewer, respond with positive and confident responses. "Yes" and "Absolutely" are preferred rather than, "Yeah" or "I think". How confident you come across and how well you articulate is very important when you meet someone. It is also important that as you go about daily activities, you dress the part. You never know who you will encounter at any given time. You could meet a potential employer or make a professional connection at Wal-Mart, the nail salon, restaurant, gym or local store. There are no limits to when and how you can meet someone. Am I suggesting that you always be suited and booted? No. However I would suggest you be well groomed and presentable at all times. You must also be mindful of your conduct and consistently display good character. You never know who is watching you and remember, there are no do-overs.

Social Media Madness

As mentioned previously, many employers use social media content to help pre-screen and qualify or disqualify candidates. The impact that it has had over the past decade is mind blowing. Used in both positive and unfortunately negative ways, social media is by-far one of the largest and most influential platforms of communications used today. You can receive uplifting motivation and inspiration and in a matter of seconds that same platform could be used to spread rumors, untruths and even display immoral behavior. I have witnessed it being used in both ways, so while it can be a highly effective tool, if used within managed parameters, if poorly managed, it can be a serious professional pitfall.

Twitter, Facebook, Instagram and other social media sites, should never be used to voice negative or defamatory content. Neither should it be used as a debating ground. It should be used to impact people in a fun and positive way by sharing positive thoughts, inspiring words, fun experiences and only posting appropriate and tasteful pictures. Unfortunately, too many young professionals are unaware of how to properly manage those tools and it can be a nightmare. My personal motto is, "Keep it clean, fun, inspiring and motivational." More than ever, employers use this advanced technology to find out whatever they want to know about candidates applying for opportunities. Students must understand that once you enter the professional scene, there is no true separation between your personal and professional life. It does not matter how many pages you create to keep things separate, you really only have one image. The two are now one. You must quickly make mature decisions about how you want to be viewed as a professional by determining what public information will ruin that image, and immediately refrain from using it. Please keep in mind that this is very serious for your professional success. I have worked for a number of companies that made final hiring decisions with public candidate information in mind. So do not taint your image.

Let the Search Begin
Phase One
Resume Preparation

The first phase is dissecting your resume. Be sure it covers the breadth of your experience without removing any valuable content. Many moons ago, job seekers were advised that a resume over one page was too much and that employers would not look at it. This train of thought forced many people to forfeit valuable content in order to keep resumes concise. Although this may have been the norm years ago, when employees were dedicated to working at one place of employment for ten to fifteen years, it is not true anymore. Over the past decade with employees changing jobs every three to four years, keeping your resume down to one page became unrealistic. You certainly do not want a wordy and redundant resume, but it should not be short of any content that would paint a good picture of you and help you shine for the potential employer.

You must also keep in mind that not only is the content important, but the presentation of your resume is critical as well. Your resume should be clear, concise, grammatically correct and easy to read with no typos, errors in dates or locations. I recall working with a number of hiring managers who frowned upon errors in a resume. They quickly associated them with candidates who did not pay attention to detail. I believe that the best approach would be to seek out resume writing assistance to ensure that the resume covers all of the necessary information. There are a number of resources that exist to help you identify the best resume type based on your career goals, as well as show you how to properly word your product without sacrificing its content.

The other very important piece is your cover letter, which many people neglect to include. A cover letter should be a brief overview of who you are, what position you are applying for, where you found the position and what skills you bring to the table that parallel with the opportunity. Your cover letter should be taken just as seriously as the resume. It should be tailored to the position you are applying for. Too often candidates send out generic cover letters and neglect to change the title of the position or details of the opportunity you are interested in. Again, you never want an employer to think that you do not pay attention to detail or that you are sending out mass resumes and have not really read their position posting.

Your job search and resume submittal should feel personal to the employer. Never omit information that the employer requests in the cover letter. Sometimes you may be asked to submit salary requirements and many people choose to omit their response because they do not know what to ask for. My general rule of thumb is to always give a salary range with a cushion of three to five thousand dollars on each end and never settle below what you realistically must have in order to survive. If they are unable to reasonably meet your salary requirements, it may not be the position for you. Do not be greedy; be honest and realistic. I would always advise indicating that salary is negotiable based on benefits. This disclaimer lets the employer know that you are open to discuss other benefits that could possibly supplement salary, such as tuition reimbursement, professional development training conferences and other benefits that have great monetary value. Many employers have a pretty robust benefits package and once you view your total benefits summary you will be able to see the monetized value of the position, which is often appealing for a new professional. What it all boils down to is you always want to give them what they are requesting so that it shows you follow directions. However, you also want to leave room for negotiation during the interview. Also, it is very important to remember when responding to job postings, if it says NO PHONE CALLS PLEASE, it is imperative that you DO NOT CALL. Career coaches or college career advisors can show you how to tactfully and discretely obtain additional information you might desire from the employer without violating the request. Phone calls against the potential employers directive, classify you as a candidate who is unable to follow directions and employers usually do not respond well to that. Remember, your polished and professional product is the first key to your new opportunity and needs to be clearly reflective of your previous experiences and properly packaged to present the best YOU!

Phase Two
The Telephone Interview

If you have successfully made it to this phase and an employer chooses to call you, realize that this is a major milestone. You are almost there. Arriving to this phase means your resume and cover letter have accomplished what they were purposed to do and now an employer is interested in seeing how well you can sell yourself over the phone. Although this is just the first telephone interview, it is still a significant part of the process. Too often candidates drop the ball at this point because they do not realize how important this phase is in relation to the big picture.

When an employer calls you the first time, there are a few things they may ask, but they are primarily seeking mutual consensus to be sure you are both on the same page regarding the current opportunity. For example, they may want to give you an overview of the company and open position, so be sure to read the website and do a little research. They may also want to be sure you have an understanding of the responsibilities and expectations of the role. You may be asked to give a brief introductory overview of your experience in relation to the position and finally they typically want to be sure you are in their ballpark with regards to salary. A general rule of thumb would be not to mention the salary during the phone interview unless the employer brings it up. Employers who are screening several candidates are trying to weed out candidates who may not be a good fit. They often base the elimination of unqualified candidates on a few things such as, poor verbal communication, inability to convey your experience in relation to the position and your personality style which include your attitude, confidence, clarity of speech, enthusiasm and articulation.

Many positions require both highly effective written and verbal communication skills. Therefore, HR professionals who usually handle the screening pay very close attention to everything during the pre-screen. Employers want to be confident that if you are considered for the next step, all of the preliminaries and disqualifying factors have been addressed before you are passed on to the hiring manager. Be confident, clear and passionate because employers can feel your energy about the opportunity. Get excited! You do want the job don't you? Well, the employer needs to hear it! Think of it this way; a person who has lost the sense of sight typically has a heightened sense of hearing. Similarly, the employer can't see you over the phone. So, they really tune in and are extra sensitive to everything you say in an attempt to get a good feel for who you are over the telephone. Honestly, you can learn quite a bit about a person through a telephone conversation and that is the intent. I like to refer to this phase as the "make it or break it" phase so practice, practice, practice! You must ace the telephone interview to get in the door.

Again, it is also important to remember that the initial call is usually the HR professional calling on behalf of the hiring manager. Be sure to sell yourself with confidence because chances are the person you are speaking with is not the final decision maker. However, they must give an accurate account of the phone call. There are a few more things you must remember. First, you are not obligated to respond to a call on the first ring. It is ok not to answer a call if you are not prepared to talk and need a few moments. I would suggest you gather yourself and then return the call. If you are driving, have a noisy background, just rolling out of bed or distracted in any way, do not feel obligated to answer on the spot. I would recommend that you let the call go to voicemail. Gather yourself and your thoughts and find a quiet place to focus and interview properly. In that same vein, it would be wise to make sure you have appropriate music on your voicemail or I would suggest no music at all. As mentioned previously, everything is subject to being judged. You never want to give the potential employer any reason to make assumptions about you in advance of meeting you personally. Once you have successfully completed this phase you are ready to prepare for the most exciting and often most intimidating phase. Depending on the position, you may have more than one in-person interview with possibly several people. It is important to prepare in advance and practice some more until you receive that call. Lastly, always email a simple thank you and express your excitement about meeting with them.

Phase Three
The In-Person Interview

Phase Three is preparation for the in-person interview, second interview or possible group interview. If you have received a call back and made it to this phase, you really need to be commended. This means you have convinced the employer that you can certainly be of value to their organization and now they would like to further pursue you. Congratulations! You have sold part of your product. It is now time to prepare and package yourself professionally and close the deal. This is usually the most exciting, yet challenging phase simply because there are a number of factors that often creep in and paralyze the jobseeker.

Most jobseekers experience a variety of emotions from nerves, anxiety, lack of confidence in face-to-face interviews and fear of being unable to clearly articulate experiences in person, versus hiding behind the telephone interview. Lastly, there is always the concern about other candidates and how you rank in comparison. A number of fleeting thoughts will flood the jobseekers mind in preparation of this phase. However, the jobseeker needs to remain calm and remember two elements. First, preparation is vital. If you prepare through practice, guidance and coaching, you can leave an interview feeling good about your responses even if you are not offered the opportunity. Knowing that you put your best foot forward is rewarding.

One of my clients was totally unaware of how to do an effective resume, what to say during a phone interview, how to dress appropriately for an interview, or even how to confidently sell herself once she got the interview. Nonetheless, she listened to my coaching and while she did not gain the first opportunity presented, she grew in confidence. After several other interviews, she received a job she loves and receives bonuses and increases often. After her first interview, she said to me, "I did not get the job, but I was more confident than ever. I felt like I was prepared and I believe that something is going to open up for me soon." She had a great perspective.

The next thing a jobseeker needs to remember is that this is a two-way interview. With all humility and respect, you should also determine if this is a place that you would like to work and invest your time. Just as the employer is trying to determine if you are someone they want to invest their resources in, you too should be confidant if you want to invest into the employer. You too are an asset. If you see yourself as an asset, you will sell yourself as an asset. You are in the best position ever NOW. Sell yourself.

Once I had a jobseeker ask me, "How do I know this particular organization is somewhere that I want to work?" My response was, "How do you know this is somewhere that you want to work?" I always advise jobseekers, to clearly be able to articulate why you want to work for a company, other than the money. If you are not able to do this, then you have a problem. Applying to jobs with salary being an important factor is one thing, but interviewing for and considering an opportunity with a company with money being the only driving factor is not wise. Money should never be the only deciding factor when considering a job opportunity. My most rewarding career opportunities happened when I took a vested interest in the company's vision, mission, core values and adopted them as my own or when I pursued my passion. Money was important but not everything. This may be easier said than done, especially when you are fresh out of college and just need a job. I get it, but if possible try to find something both personally and financially rewarding. Whatever your initial situation, remember to avoid taking an opportunity just for the money.

Another important part of this process is doing your due diligence. Doing research on the company you are interested in working for is very important. You need to know as much as you can about your potential employer. Another few simple interview reminders is to always bring several copies of your resume with you to your interview. I would suggest three copies at minimum. It is acceptable to ask the person scheduling the interview how many people you will be meeting with so that you can be well prepared with resumes.

As you are preparing for the day of the interview, you must be on time. It is *very* important to remember to arrive ten minutes early. Tardiness to an interview is not acceptable and there is absolutely no excuse. You must also be sure you are not on the phone when you arrive and that your phone is completely silenced. Unless someone is deathly ill, there is no emergency more important during the hour of an interview. The employer should have your undivided attention. The other very important thing to remember is that the receptionist, also referred to as the gatekeeper is watching you. This person is not there just to welcome you in and offer you coffee, but he or she is unofficially a part of the interview process. Be cordial, but avoid small talk. Bring a book and remain engaged until it is time to meet the hiring manager. Entertaining small talk often opens up cans of worms because you can become too comfortable and let your guard down. I recall my days as the recruiter/hiring manager handling interviews. I would always ask the receptionist to give me her take on the candidate. It was always very helpful feedback in the decision making process. This person's opinion is certainly not the final say, but it certainly adds value, so be nice to the gatekeeper.

Once you are greeted and invited into the interview conference room, the employer will often lead the interview explaining what will occur during the interview and open up with the first question. It is important to listen, process and answer accordingly. Do not cut interviewers off by being too anxious to respond to their questions. Neither should you go off on a tangent by responding to everything except what has been asked of you. It is ok to think about your response before you speak. During the course of the interview, you may be asked questions requiring a direct response or open dialogue may happen so you can feel free to add value as necessary. Do not ever feel under pressure to respond without thinking out your answers.

Also, always bring something to write with and on. I have always brought a professional portfolio with pad and pen to write down questions and take notes of pertinent information that I may want to refer to later. I would always ask the employer if it was ok for me to take notes. It was never an issue and came across quite studious. This is also an excellent way to note questions for the employer once the interview is complete and to read for future reference.

Once the official interview starts, the employer will usually tell you about the company and may even ask if you know anything about the organization. So again, before you arrive for the interview make sure that you check out their website. It is critical that you have some information on the company for two reasons. First, employers are leery about candidates who do not take time to learn about the company. Secondly, why would you want to work for a company you know nothing about? Checking out the website is for your benefit as well. Remember, this is a two-way interview and the best decisions are made with the most information. Therefore, you need to know all you can to create a platform for dialogue when it is your turn to speak. All of what you learn will eventually help you to make an informed decision about accepting an offer if one is presented.

Interviewers will always ask you to tell them about yourself. This is not a time to ramble on about personal information. Remember, less is more. I would only advise you to briefly share any experience in relation to the position which you have applied, a little about your personality and your work style. Do not tell them if you have children, whether you are married or not or any unnecessary personal information. Also, they are not allowed to ask you. The follow-up question is usually a request to walk them through your resume, if you have experience. What that means is tell us about your experiences you have on paper. This is the time for you to humbly boast on your accomplishments and experiences and use every opportunity to inject critical information that they may not have asked, but you think would be beneficial for them to know. I remember on several occasions being asked about my management style. Not only would I explain my style, but I would also include examples of times where I felt I made good decisions in my management roles. This may not have been the basis of the original question, but I could see the interviewers' eyebrows raise when I shared with them answers that gave them information to help in their decision making. I would encourage you to share all the good stuff.

In the interview, you must sell what makes you unique. At this point you are in the final stages and most likely you have at least one competitor. Therefore, you must convey your value without hesitation. It is critical that you give your all. Lastly, be sure to ask questions before the interview is complete. I always suggest that you ask about the person who was in the position before you. It would be helpful for you to know why the position is vacant and what you could do differently than the previous person who held the position. I would always ask about your supervisor's management style. It is important to know the personality and work style of people you are working with. I would also ask, "If hired, what could I accomplish within the next 30 days, to confirm that you hired the right person for the job?" You always want to assure the employer you are ready to hit the ground running and excited about making an immediate impact. Lastly, *never* ever share your negative experiences or feelings about a previous supervisor. Always find positive things to highlight, even if it was not the greatest experience. The interview can be tricky but you can handle it.

Ultimately, for new graduates, it is important to unpack your total work history. You need to include paid, as well as unpaid jobs and successfully incorporate all of your experiences and transferable skills relating them to the position you are interviewing for; even those you feel have no value. Transferable skills are skills that may not be identical to what the employer is asking for, but are still in the same vein. For example, if the position requires that you handle petty cash, but the only experience you can relate is your babysitting job where you were responsible for allocating money to take care of the kids, that would be considered a transferable skill. As a new professional with minimal experience, being able to communicate transferrable skills is going to be important.

"I would encourage any new professional just starting out in their career to try to find a job doing what you love, and do not embark upon a career just for money. Do something you are passionate about and you will always be fulfilled. When you do what you love, and perfect it, you will always walk away feeling rewarded."

LaTonia Rush
Certified Life Coach

"During my job search I was getting numerous job interviews but no call backs for job offers. After receiving career coaching from Selise and learning effective ways to answer questions during the interview process, I finally received a job offer!"

Delisha Michelle Clemons
Engineering Technical Specialist

"During your interview, leave them with the impression that you are committed. Strongly pursue positions that you want. Be yourself and bring things to the table that will make you stand out. Your originality and personality will be one of the things that will be remembered by future employers. Lastly, be humble because nothing is owed to you.

Austin P. Taylor
Mechanical Engineering Intern

Phase Four
After The Interview

Phase four is the final and simplest phase, but probably equally as important as the others. This phase includes follow-up and thank you notes to all of the parties you met during the process. I know it may not seem important, but a little thank you goes a long way. I personally live by that rule and have shared it with others who have called me to say thanks for that bit of insight. Follow-up thank you notes, show great professional etiquette and have always been the icing on the cake or the deal sealer for me. I remember telling the story of how I went from five dollars to five thousand in five minutes. My very first contract I received doing some professional development training was not given to me because of my consulting resume, or because I had no clients to endorse my work at that time. However, after a PowerPoint presentation on what I thought I could do for the client and explaining why I thought I was the best person for the opportunity, I ran to Starbucks to purchase two five dollar gift cards and put them in thank you notes for both Directors who were at the presentation. I made sure to deliver the cards that day and less than 24 hours later, I was offered the contract. One might see that gesture as a bit much, but I saw it as an investment into my future consulting business. Needless to say I secured a few additional contracts with that company soon thereafter. I have also coached several other clients on using that same approach and it worked. Am I telling you to buy a five dollar Starbucks gift card for everyone at every interview? No, I am not. You must decide what's worth the investment. However, regardless of what you do, you must attempt to stand out and always send thank you notes to everyone you interview with. The method could be different for every interviewer. For example, I have sent emails to all of the parties who I interviewed with, but only one gift card to the hiring manager. There are times when I would just send emails or leave thank you cards for all parties with the receptionist before leaving the vicinity. Regardless of the method you choose, the key is to be sure it is done promptly and effectively. Be sure to get all names, titles and proper spelling of who you met with. Also, remember to take notes in the interview referencing some of the things each interviewer stated as particularly important to them so you can personalize the thank you. I know this seems tedious, but it sets you apart because not everyone thinks it is necessary, but these are methods I have used for years and they work.

When each phase is successfully executed you can guarantee an opportunity is on the way. I have often met with jobseekers who had not taken the time to properly assess where they were in the process, but were adamant that they needed a refaced resume because they were not securing job opportunities. However, what I have found after completing an assessment is that they had a very well put together product and did receive call backs. Sometimes, they did receive second and even third interviews, only to find that another candidate was selected. If this happens more than once, it would behoove the jobseeker to evaluate all phases of the search process to properly identify where the disconnect may be. Proper guidance and coaching as you evaluate each step will help you to identify where you need help getting unstuck. No matter what you do, remember that each phase is important and necessary as you secure your opportunity.

Chapter 3

Remove YOU
Retaining The Opportunity

"Do you wish to be great? Then begin by being. Do you desire to construct a vast and lofty fabric? Think first about the foundations of humility. The higher your structure is to be, the deeper must be its foundation." - Saint Augustine

Believe it or not, getting the job is easier than keeping the job; especially when you are first starting your career. Too many young professionals miss this critical part of the process simply because of what you do not know. Many of you have plenty of classroom knowledge, but very little corporate sense and it is not your fault. You cannot be held accountable for what you have not been told. There is certainly a need for training on corporate decorum.

Professionalism in the workplace is such a broad topic that any attempt to cover every area would be impossible. I will simply identify a few common professional pitfalls that I have witnessed both new and seasoned professionals get caught in, only to end up clueless and jobless. I do not want that to happen to you. While pursuing and securing the opportunity requires that you market and sell you, retaining the opportunity is going to require that you remove "you."

Your focus will be on learning, growing and developing in a new environment. It is now time to be coachable, teachable, humble and open to being groomed for your future. You will now be prepared for professional advancement. Remember, if you think you "got it," you still do not "get it." My desire is now that you have successfully made it through the process with opportunities being offered, you will not only get a great job, but you will be equipped to keep, and thrive in it.

The Paradigm Shift

It is vitally important that new professionals understand the major difference between the college environment and the corporate environment. There are different codes and certainly a whole different set of rules. This can be a major professional pitfall if a new graduate is unaware of how to think and operate. For example, in college, friendships are promoted and actually needed for survival. College also encourages students to be vocal and outspoken about their opinions and concerns. Students are graded on class participation and expected to offer feedback in many instances. However, in the corporate arena it is quite the opposite. Developing personal or intimate relationships and friendships, other than corporate relationships, is not celebrated or encouraged as much and neither are the opinions and input of new inexperienced college grads. Please understand that I am not trying to discourage you from developing professional relationships in the workplace; nor am I trying to discourage you from finding your voice and providing valuable input when given the opportunity. However, what I am trying to do is prevent you from being shunned at the start of your career because of poor professional choices. When you enter the corporate world as a new professional, the safe zone for the first 30-90 days is to be still, silent and observant as you learn your job and the environment. I remember working with this one young professional who never said much and chose her words wisely and when she spoke, people listened. She was perceived as wise beyond her years. It is perfectly fine to be quiet and observe. Many mentors and seasoned professionals have helped me develop in that area.

ALL Work and NO Play

The college environment is generally where new students develop a number of relationships that either validate their need to belong, fulfill the desire to be a part of something larger and more meaningful than them, or endorse their desire to finally express their individuality with limited restrictions. It is a no judgment zone amongst their peers where they feel safe and accepted. New college students are always looking to connect. Many students who have never been independent, seek to explore life on a different level with relationships that are cultivated over several years, and that will eventually lead to lifetime friendships. Whether it be your suite mates, new classmates, sorority sisters or fraternity brothers, developing relationships, particularly friendships, are vital to most college students. On the contrary, friendships are not celebrated as much in the corporate world unless you are able to successfully develop boundaries, which is usually not the case for young professionals.

From my 25 years of observation, friendships in the workplace that are not properly managed often impact professionalism. Many times there is a comfort level developed that results in guards being let down. Employees start engaging in things like frequent lunch dates, happy hours and social gatherings. Initially, it seems innocent until it develops into cliques or unhealthy intimate relationships that eventually impact the organization. These relationships have a tendency to encourage conversations that usually result in unproductive gripes or gossip about leadership, company policy, co-workers in other departments or things that make them disgruntled, which in turn causes division within the organization and in many instances negatively impacts productivity. Can friendships be developed in the workplace and not result in the above? Yes, absolutely! However, it requires professional maturity which is rare with new professionals.

Most young professionals have not worked long enough to understand how to navigate the muddy waters of professional politics and until that happens, it would be wise to seek out professional associates *only* and not friendships. You want to connect with colleagues that can enhance your experience within the organization and help you grow professionally. Stay away from complainers, gossipers and trouble stirrers. I am not suggesting that you work constantly shielded behind closed doors or operate in a silo. As a matter of fact, I support you ingratiating into the culture. I just encourage you to understand how to properly engage workplace relationships. As an HR professional, I rarely received invites to lunches or happy hours unless the intent was to pick my brain about something happening in the office and those instances were minimal. I must admit it was very challenging at the start of my career simply because I love interacting with people, but I learned a hard quick lesson and never had a problem again. I accepted that I was hired as a professional to do a job and not make friends. I was responsible for championing the company's vision while advocating for staff needs which was a balancing act. Friendships in the workplace, especially in my role, would make that process very difficult. I learned quickly that my career was more important than work friendships. Now, did I go to lunch occasionally? Of course, but I was very strategic to choose my company and conversation wisely. It will not be easy to make this shift in thinking at first, but trust me, professional relationships rather than friendships are wiser and healthier.

It Is JUST Business

Learning how to conduct yourself corporately, particularly in the boardroom, especially when things get heated, is a very important skill that certainly takes time and patience to develop. Knowing when to speak, what to say and what not to say, as well as learning not to take things personal is also important.

Over the years, I have learned, and I am still learning, that sometimes silence is platinum. While it may take time to learn the art of silence when first transitioning, it is definitely something every new professional needs to learn quickly in order to earn a trusted voice at the table. Another exciting, yet intimidating part of your transition, will be the opportunity to grow professionally in a number of ways to include being asked to participate in or maybe even facilitate meetings or focus groups. It may seem intimidating at first, but this is an excellent opportunity for you to grow and become more professionally engaged if handled properly. These meetings will include everything from impromptu departmental meetings to organizational meetings. Regardless of the meeting purpose, it is important to know how to conduct yourself. The first thing you must do is earn a trusted and sound voice at the table before providing too much input, which could take a few meetings to accomplish. I have witnessed new professionals who chose to speak at meetings too soon only to share information that had no relevance and held no weight. This persons attempt to speak at subsequent meetings resulted in everyone wondering what was going to come out of their mouth next. As we know, college usually encourages students to participate in debate clubs, lead group assignments, participate in class discussions, voice your opinions and give continual feedback on a number of issues. You are required to participate to maintain a good grade. However, it is quite the opposite in corporate. You are encouraged, as a new professional, to be a sponge and absorb and learn as much as you can before you see the need to offer input. Honestly, how much value can you really add if you have only been in the organization for a few weeks? Less is definitely more when newly entering the workforce. This is your opportunity to learn. If an opportunity presents itself for you to contribute, be sure to evaluate your comment before giving input by asking yourself is this comment necessary or do I just desire to fill dead space? Will my input add value to the discussion or just be another piggy back comment? Is there anyone else around the table who can contribute to this statement?

Finally, the most important question you must ask yourself is, "Will I regret having said something after I make the statement?" Again, I am not trying to discourage you from sharing your voice, but I have witnessed many young professionals make contributions that added no value only to regret it later feeling as if the comment could have been avoided. When you just desire to contribute, but do not add real value, you lose credibility and it takes time to rebuild your own personal confidence and the confidence of others. It only takes one "foot in mouth" incident. I have been there and it is not a good feeling. To avoid this, you must seek to contribute positively with the right posture and tone and remember the key is quality not quantity; less is definitely more. There is something to be said about those who listen more than they speak. Newton once stated, "It is better to remain silent and be thought a fool than to open your mouth and remove all doubt." Personal opinions are frowned upon when you are too new to have concrete contributions. Listen, learn and only contribute as necessary. Another simple key to remember is when you are invited to the boardroom, check your emotions at the door. There is absolutely no room for personal feelings or being easily offended in the boardroom, just facts.

If you desire to grow, you must also learn to accept constructive feedback without offense. Develop thick skin and do not take everything so personally. Honestly, this can be challenging. I have witnessed and been a part of heated discussions where no one wanted to back down resulting in no resolve. However, I have also witnessed and admired professionals who could attend a meeting, be placed on the hot seat and leave the meeting without a chip on their shoulder because they did not take anything personally. Those leaders learned how to handle hot topics with a cool temper. It was all just business. As you grow professionally, a number of opportunities will expose you to situations that will require you to remove your emotions from the equation. While it may not always be easy, the sooner you mature in that area, the sooner higher-level opportunities will be offered to you.

Along your journey you will interact with a number of Professionals. Many will be more seasoned than you and may feel the need to correct or guide you even when you have not asked for it. Although not always invited, seasoned professionals usually have great wisdom to offer, but many times it will not be packaged with a bow. However, if you learn the art of hearing the truth in every situation and removing your emotions you are well on your way to professional maturity. Developing this skill takes time, but again the sooner you can master that, the quicker you will see manager level opportunities come your way. Develop thick skin and do not take everything so personally.

> *"One of my first mistakes as a young professional was not taking advantage of the wisdom and guidance offered by senior leaders. It is very important that you soak up the knowledge of the individuals who are experts in your field. You should also learn the difference between constructive feedback and criticism. Early in my career I perceived every correction given as negative criticism, but as I have grown professionally, I later realized that most, if not all, corrections were good feedback and once applied, helped me to function at my highest potential."*

Willie F. Diggs II- LBSW, MSW
Assistant Professor
Department of Social Work, Counseling and Psychology

Learn the Rhythm

I remember hearing a simple demonstration on how important it is for everyone in an orchestra to know the piece being played, as well as their assigned part in order to keep the tempo and rhythm. One person who is off beat or out of sync could throw everything completely off. The demonstration was a simple way to explain how important it is for any new person, in any organization, to carefully assess the environment to determine how to effectively inject new ideas. Many new professionals, who do not choose to first learn the rhythm or the culture of an organization, often throw off the tempo and rhythm with an innocent attempt to shift the culture.

Many young professionals are smart, excited and ready to hit the ground running, but I would caution against presumptuous attempts to push change too soon. It would be wise to study your environment and learn the organizations pulse. Your ideas may be great and your heart, motives and intentions may be pure, but if the timing isn't right, it could really throw a monkey wrench in things. Learning the rhythm can help you fall in line with an easy, seamless and unobtrusive transition simply because there is so much you cannot see with the naked eye. There are a number of unspoken codes in every organization that you should be aware of. It would also be wise to learn who the players are. Next, you need to understand the vision, where the company is headed with its strategic direction and what challenges they are facing. It only makes sense to learn the culture of an organization before making attempts to implement any type of change. My advice would be to keep silent with all suggestions for the first 30 days. Learn the lay of the land, ask questions, listen to the common theme and pay attention. It will make it easier for you to navigate without overstepping boundaries or stepping on toes. The worst thing a new professional can do is enter an organization with unharnessed energy, excited about implementing change or suggestions that the organization is really not ready to receive. I have witnessed a number of excited young professionals who were ready to move forward with amazing ideas, but found themselves connected to organizations that were stuck on the cusp of change, but had not decided to move forward. So many organizations have a desire to grow to another level and even have the human capital with the right skills and knowledge at their disposal, but because of fear of change or not knowing how to capitalize on people around them, they miss major opportunities. This scenario can be very frustrating to new professionals. Many young professionals are innovative, forward thinking and ready to put plans into action. This can often create conflict if an organization is not very open to change, even though it may be evident there is a need. Also, this can create conflict if seasoned professionals, who may be set in their ways, are not very receptive to change. If not approached correctly, both of these dynamics can make the implementation of new ideas seem almost impossible.

My personal rule of thumb, when entering a new organization, is to enter with a "How can I help" attitude and then learn as you grow. Make every effort to understand the company dynamics. Learn and understand the vision and mission of the organization. Identify insufficiencies that exist in your area of expertise and then figure out how you can be an asset and not a liability by filling in the gaps. Also, read as much as you can about the organizations history and goals. Learn the company points of pain and how you can assist in resolving those issues. Learn all you can about your department and your direct supervisor and see how you can fit in and effectively support the departmental goals. As you can see there is a lot for you to learn and do when you start a new job so do not allow resistance to frustrate you. You are the new kid on the block and your goal is to gain experience, learn and grow; not change the company. Be patient and only provide suggestions as you learn the culture and when asked. There will be plenty of opportunities to make suggestions and recommendations in the future, but first things first: learn the rhythm.

You also need to learn the heart of the leader and determine what is important to him or her. This person may be responsible for the overall success of your department or the entire company. Therefore knowing the leader's heart helps you to stay committed even when policies, procedures and directives do not make sense or are difficult to accept. Learning your direct supervisor's rhythm is very wise as well. When you learn the character, personality and leadership style of the person you are assigned to support, it will make for an easier, more productive relationship. Seek to understand how they operate and think. Learn what is important to them and what is of no relevance. Simply put, learn to think like they think. Try to stay one step ahead of them at all times. Do not make assumptions on what they want or how they want things done until you have completely learned them and their style. It is always best to ask and clarify.

When I learned that one of my Directors was married to a retired General, it started to make all the sense in the world. I began to understand why she was always "driving in my lane." She was a great person, but she would forward me a request or give me directives and end up somehow handling part or all of them before I could even process the task. I wondered was I not getting to it quick enough. But when I realized she was completing some tasks even before she mentioned them to me, I thought there is more to this. One day I requested to meet with her to discuss my concern only to find that because she was so accustomed to handling everything herself, to include the household, kids etc., in her husband's absence, by default she would naturally jump right in and start making things happen. Also, it did not help that she had a very particular way about getting things done. Once I understood this about her, it all made sense and our working relationship immediately shifted. Things were so much easier. Learning the rhythm of your leader and how they are wired is critical to your success.

It is also important to understand their leadership style and personality type. There are a number of personality tests that you can request your leader take and the results will tell you quite a bit about how they operate. I would suggest you ask your supervisor if they have taken one and request to see the results. Once you see how they scored, it will help you determine how to effectively interact with them. These tests are often given to both parties and once the results are reviewed, it usually helps to foster healthy work relationships. I have watched wise employees discover the type of leader they were working with and adjust to their needs. I have also witnessed unwise employees who create tension and conflict between themselves and the employer because they are insubordinate and refuse to be flexible or learn the rhythm.

"Learning the established rhythm of an organization will have an impact on your success in that organization. Without knowing the

established rhythm, your talent can be more disruptive than beneficial."

Pastor A.E. Wheeler

Serve Now, Lead Later

During my career, I have witnessed far too many new professionals who adopt an entitlement mentality that says, "I have committed countless classroom hours, study hours, sleepless nights, and thousands of dollars in student loans towards my education; therefore my expectation is that I would have the red carpet rolled out upon graduation with job offers in my field knocking at my door." The harsh reality is that this unrealistic expectation will set you up for disappointment every time.

When we consider the college graduate rate, the highly saturated job market and how many students graduate each year competing amongst themselves as well as other seasoned professionals, we must resolve that landing the dream job or even a job remotely close to your major after graduation just may not happen. According to research conducted by Forbes Magazine, only 27 percent of college graduates have a job related to their major upon graduation. However, landing an opportunity that can properly position you to pursue your career and eventually secure that dream job is highly probable, given the right coaching and guidance. There are always exceptions to the rule, but depending upon your degree that is not typically the norm. Most all successful professionals will tell you that they did not secure their dream job right out of college, without first working in other less desirable entry level positions. Therefore, it is important to be realistic about the climate of this job market in order to stay encouraged as you pursue opportunities. It is equally important to know that opportunities must be earned. No one is entitled to anything.

I have found in researching and speaking with a number of hiring managers, CEOs and leaders, the number one turnoff when hiring a new professional is the attitude of entitlement. Too many new professionals are ready to be on the fast track to success making withdrawals before any deposits. I am convinced that the media has skewed the thinking of many new professionals by painting an unrealistic picture of what equals success in the corporate world. Too often an illusion is painted that one has "arrived" once you secure a corner office, electronic gadgets, flexibility and a seat at the table. What many fail to realize is those perks are earned through countless hours of sweat equity and often come with a high price, like late work nights, constant off the clock requests and high margins for performance.

I remember the first job I had with a Blackberry and laptop. Although I loved the work I did, those items were like leashes. Some days I felt like I no longer had a personal life. Those gadgets were buzzing all the time. I was often frustrated wondering if I could turn them in, but as a part of the management team I had no choice. Ironically enough, the stress level at that job was high and I had a brain aneurysm shortly after my departure. Can I blame the company for my sickness? Of course not, but the level of responsibility, expectation and pressure certainly contributed to my stress level. I encourage you, as you ambitiously pursue roles with that level of responsibility, please be aware that it is not always what it is cracked up to be. It is certainly great to pursue advancement, but everything has its price so make sure you are ready. Unfortunately, I have witnessed far too many new professionals enter organizations with unharnessed energy that must be channeled in order to ensure success. Lacking wisdom, they run past skilled and seasoned professionals who they should be relying on for help. Later, they find themselves blackballed by those same professionals who have put in countless years of service and refuse to just step aside. The unfortunate thing is that many of these seasoned professionals would be great coaches and mentors for the younger professionals if they chose to leverage the professional relationships and not try and railroad them. As a new professional you must learn to acquiesce. The worst thing you can do is get labeled with the taboo word "entitlement." Way too often one would look at the positions of title and stature not taking into account the level of responsibility connected with those roles.

Leaders must be professional, disciplined, dedicated, loyal, committed, have character, integrity and resilience just to name a few. Those qualities are learned, developed and tested through experience and time. Therefore you could not possibly have them upon entering your first real or even second solid job opportunity; it takes years of grooming. I would advise young professionals entering any organization to take some time to observe the leadership and identify someone who can be a mentor to you as you grow professionally.

I have interviewed countless young professionals desiring close to the top end of the salary range with little to no experience except their summer internship, who join organizations perk driven. I have often wondered where is the mentality that is willing to just support, serve and be grateful that an opportunity has even been extended given the competition. It is critical that new professionals understand what it means to "pay your dues." To enter an organization scoping out the next opportunity for promotion is the wrong approach. Prudent young professionals should understand that the greatest leaders had to first serve well. In due season, you will be afforded leadership opportunities within the organization. First it will require seeds of serving faithfully and diligently. Leadership privileges must be earned and that does not happen overnight. There are seasons of testing that must take place in the areas of integrity, loyalty, diligence, faithfulness and proven technical skills, before you can earn a seat at the table.

It is important to know that every renowned soloist was a back-up singer at one point and every CEO reported to someone at some point. One of the greatest benefits of serving is the opportunity for your skills to be sharpened, honed and developed during that time. You will never be successful entering the corporate arena with your eyes fixated on advancement. However, if you are offered an opportunity to serve on the leadership team early on in your career in any capacity, count it a privilege. I have been in corporate for 20 years and actively a part of ministry for almost all of my life and I can recall, in both arenas, countless days when I cleaned toilets, emptied trash, visited nursing homes, sat at the reception desk as a manager and just simply did whatever was necessary. I did not realize at that time that there was great value in those moments of serving which developed character, humility and dedication that I probably would not have learned any other way. I would not trade those moments for anything. Focus on serving and your leadership days will be closer than you might think.

Serving With Integrity

Whatever you put out, you can almost expect to get back. Therefore, I always encourage new and seasoned professionals to put out good energy, display a positive attitude and always offer genuine and sincere support in anticipation of a great return when it is your time to lead. Some days it can be painless. I will be the first to admit that it can also be a very difficult task at times. Especially if you are working for a challenging leader or you really do not understand or agree with their decisions. I have been there. Respect, honor and compliance with your superior, regardless of whether you agree or disagree, is the key. Anything other than that is insubordination and frowned upon in any professional setting. Many professionals do not realize that you may respectfully disagree. It is how you do it.

> *I am a firm believer that what you sow when you serve, will determine what you reap when you lead.*

I once consulted with a company where the owner and sales manager just did not see eye-to-eye. The sales manager totally disagreed with many of the decisions the owner made. I always reminded him that the owner was the final authority and what he said was the gospel. I did give suggestions to both parties on how they could better work together. At the end of the day, even if they couldn't come to a happy medium, submission to the leader with the right posture and attitude was expected. The sales manager's posture made it difficult because he refused to learn his leader's rhythm. New professionals must remember that one of their primary reasons for being in the position they have been hired for is to support their leader and make them look good at all times.

Your success is highly dependent upon their success. It does not matter how much you think you know or how innovative and technologically savvy you may be in comparison to your leader, you must not lose sight of the fact that you are there to support and serve and it must be done with the right attitude.

There are a number of key principles you must learn quickly. First, you should never seek to expose or usurp the authority of those in leadership. Many new professionals are well versed and trained to lead and manage and unafraid to jump right in. I have heard the millennial generation being referred to as "A generation that does not know what they can't do." Therefore, it is no surprise that they are ready to get in, roll their sleeves up and hit the ground running with lots of zeal and ideas. However, I caution you to be sure to stay in sync with your leader and not get ahead of them. There is much to be learned from their wisdom and experience and there is always an order to things. I often encourage young professionals to think outside the box, but advise them to stay within the lines. It is really not a hard concept to grasp because many leaders are looking for what I refer to as a "support partner." They are looking for someone who they can rely on to bounce ideas around with and get a fresh perspective, as well as someone who is coachable and easy to mentor. Be innovative, creative and forward thinking, but do it within reasonable parameters.

There will be times when you may be able to see their shortcomings and insecurities, but that is for you to encourage them and support them, not to judge or criticize their leadership style or decisions. You have been trusted with their frailties, not to expose them, but to keep them covered. You are assigned to guard them. When your leader is successful, everyone is successful. Also, do not be offended if you think you know a better way to approach something and they may not be receptive. You are still too new to really add value which may make them very reluctant to even hear your input or feedback at first. However, if approached correctly, with wisdom, humility and proper timing, you could be setting yourself up for amazing professional success and relationship with your leader. I have experienced it.

I recall working with several professional leaders early in my career before I understood this concept and I screwed up royally. I was always able to be trusted, but my issue was I knew it all. After being trained under some very sound business men and women, it eventually made sense. It took time but I got it. I want you to avoid that professional pitfall. Over time, I began to develop bonds where my leaders could trust me, but it always started with me humbly and respectfully honoring their position and listening to instruction regardless of how much I thought I knew. Be patient and humbly submit to those who are in leadership positions.

I learned a lot of lessons during those times about how to work in tandem with my leader and not against the grain. I yielded amazing results after I understood how to tread lightly, offer valuable feedback and listen a lot before speaking. Most importantly, I learned that my time in leadership would be coming and I wanted to reap a good harvest because I had good seed in the ground. I never wanted to wonder if I was being challenged in any of my leadership roles as a direct result of my inability to be faithful, or because of how I treated or failed in my service to my leader. Please know that we will make mistakes as we learn and grow, but you want to avoid planting any bad seeds.

As I matured professionally, I can recall working with

one professional who hired me and immediately saw me as her partner. Although she was Senior Vice President of HR and I was only being hired in as an assistant manager, she immediately recognized the value I could add and began referring to me as her HR partner. I thought it was an honor to be viewed in that light and I was determined to be the best partner I could. We disagreed at times, but I always respectfully shared my opinions and concerns. As professionals, we always came to a happy medium. I think we both grew as a result. Despite the privilege of being given an unmerited seat at the table, I always respected her role and her final authority. I also recall working for the Chief Operating Officer of one organization and she too invited me to be on the leadership team for the division. I remember it as if it were yesterday. During my interview for the head HR position she asked, "What if you did not agree with me on a decision, how would you respond?" My response was honest and simple, "If I did not agree with you, I would respectfully express my concern, reasons why I had a difference in opinion and suggest other options for resolve." I further expressed that I would never disagree or be combative in public. You could tell she was impressed with the response. Needless to say, while she was a very smart woman, I later came to learn that she was a hot-head, who was quick to make decisions that were not always well thought out, often controversial and easy to disagree with, hence the reason for the question. However, we always seemed to reason to a point of sensible action on an issue. Again, the point here is that her respect for my contribution resulted in a seat at the table, but the major key was handling the situation properly.

You must remember that no one wants to hire someone

consistently combative or posing opposition. You must be able to sell yourself on being amicable and harmonious despite challenges that may arise. If you are still working on that, you have time.

The key to corporate success in serving is to remember it is not just that we serve but how we serve. Simply serving is not enough. You must serve with a positive attitude of excellence. You should always be looking for ways to lighten the load. Am I saying that it is easy? Absolutely not! Many leaders are still learning themselves so be patient as you both grow together. I am sure every person reading this book at some point will aspire to be a leader or become one by default in some capacity, so it is imperative that you remember you are in training.

> *"I have learned that maintaining my integrity, especially when dealing with a difficult boss allows their position of defense and lack of trust to be removed, which has the power to create and promote a healthy and non-hostile environment."*
> *Tia Turner- College Student*

Serve On Purpose

"I hate my job!" Words you can expect to hear from a person who has been working somewhere for ten minutes or even ten years and they have no passion towards their position; neither do they receive any fulfillment from it. If you are not careful you could find yourself in this same place feeling unfulfilled. Of course you will always have aspects of a job you do not like; it comes with the territory. However, if you are always unhappy, complaining about your work, and miserable 80-90% of the time, that is a problem. I often caution people on working for organizations where the core values do not line up with your own personal core values or there is no vision for your growth or positioning. There must be real purpose in you being there. You must remember you have been hired for a number of reasons, both obvious and others not so obvious. You are not just there to do a job. You are on an assignment.

An assignment is specific work that you have been charged to accomplish that extends far beyond the scope of your job description and daily work duties. Which in my experience are often associated with a greater spiritual purpose. You may be gifted to encourage, so your assignment may be to encourage staff in challenging situations that need to know they can make it. Your gift may be to offer wisdom to someone who is making a decision that requires wise counsel. Whatever your gift may be, you are assigned to the company to do more than type letters or develop software.

Typically when you acknowledge your assignment you will notice staff members will start gravitating towards you in need of what you have to share. So whether it is someone you have the wisdom to instruct, or a skill that you have been trained to implement, YOU have been assigned to do it. Seeing the job as an assignment makes it so much more meaningful. It prompts purpose and it becomes more rewarding to go to work every day. I personally believe you are assigned to that particular organization ultimately for two reasons, to be a light and a sponge. As a light, you are an extension of hope to those you work with daily. Your assignment is to be the conduit that is being used to reach those within your sphere of influence.

As a light, you are responsible for finding ways to show

kindness in times of uncertainty when people need to know there is hope. As a sponge, you must soak up all you can in knowledge and experience to use for a greater purpose outside of your current job. While I was taking corporate training classes titled, "How To Be A Highly Effective Speaker," I remember learning professional speaking techniques that I use today as a motivational speaker and minister. I immediately saw the benefit of applying this practical advice. You must realize that this is more than just a job, it is an assignment. With a job you go in to work daily to complete basic tasks and projects with the mentality that I am going to do my best and my ultimate reward every week or two is my paycheck. However, the approach towards an assignment is a bit different. First, you understand that the greatest reward is not your paycheck, although we must work to live. When you see your job as an assignment you are looking to not only accomplish basic daily tasks for monetary gain, but you are looking to serve, support and seek out opportunities to make a lasting impression in the lives of those you interact with daily during your time there.

Every gesture you make towards someone in need of encouragement, motivation or a word of hope is really what solidifies your position. I am not telling you to spend all day encouraging others and not doing your work. It should naturally be a part of your work day. Every employee should help to maintain company morale. I like to refer to an assignment as purposeful positioning to accomplish a task that you have been charged to complete.

I remember working at an organization that obviously had major needs. Immediately upon arrival, I began to meditate and I prayed to determine who or what was my assignment. Approximately 24 hours later, it was made crystal clear to me that the people at the job needed to know there was hope. I had several impromptu meetings, not planned by me, in my office, encouraging various members of the team. As HR they were comfortable with me being a safe trustworthy sounding board. I did everything from helping staff with work related issues, to a number of personal issues. A young man was having personal challenges with family and he would come to my office to get guidance. He knew I was a minister and needed a safe place to share. I was able to be a voice of encouragement and wise counsel for him and his family. I was not hired specifically for that, but it was a part of the assignment. I recall another time there was a young lady who was aware of my faith and often sought me out for constant guidance and direction. One day she needed prayer for her husband and family for a job opportunity so I encouraged her and we prayed. We talked all the time, but this day she wanted to pray. He got the job!

I can share numerous stories like that. My point is, you must quickly understand why you are there because people are depending on you for a word of hope and encouragement; a smile or a prayer. You are not just there to fulfill a job description, attend a meeting or prepare a report. I am not merely suggesting that you become a counselor neglecting your daily work responsibilities, but I believe people are more important than paper. Therefore, regardless of the need you have been hired to fulfill, do it. And although your assignment may differ in nature from what I shared, it does not change the fact that you are at that job for a higher reason. For new professionals, I would not really encourage personal meetings until you have mastered the art of creating boundaries. Do know that there is something specific you are called to do. You will know it when it presents itself. If you sit still long enough and observe the needs around you, you will start to see what you are called to do.

Realize that wherever you are positioned professionally, it is not an accident. You were purposed to work and serve at that specific company and under the perfect person so they could help groom, grow, develop and refine your character for future positioning. While it may be a mutually beneficial relationship, you must be sure to approach it with a student mentality, open to learning and being coachable. You will never have learned enough. Consider yourself a lifetime student and be open to teachable moments. As mentioned in the previous section, you have been assigned to work for that person because they are seasoned in an area that you must mature, grow and develop in. They have been placed in a position of leadership over you for a reason, so while serving, you must learn to respectfully submit to authority no matter the dynamic.

Many of you are very savvy and much more innovative than people who will hire you primarily because of how technologically advanced the world is becoming. However, whether you are younger and maybe more knowledgeable in one area or another, it does not negate the fact that they are still your leader. That does not mean that you are not allowed to suggest a more effective way to carry out a task or implement a new process or procedure, but it is your approach that makes the difference. Be very careful of your approach when you need clarity or have a difference of opinion. You are not expected not to have your own ideas, but it is all about how you present them. Learn to comply and not complain. Too often we are quick to voice our valid and often justifiable personal feelings or we feel like we have the "right" to share our discontent. Oftentimes, we are driven by emotion and not facts. While you may have valid concerns, the posture you take when you voice those concerns is important. Remember, respect is critical for professional growth.

I remember working for a lady who was very nice. She was certainly more seasoned and I was honored that she saw me as an asset and often referred to me as her HR partner. It made me feel great to know that she saw me in that light and although we often had differing opinions, we really balanced each other and worked well as a team. I would get upset that she allowed certain staff to treat our department with disregard and in my opinion, she did not handle things like I thought she should. As time went on, I learned that she operated in wisdom by handling things with diplomacy and tact. She was professional enough to know that we were not in a battle with other departments. We were there to get a task done in an amicable and peaceful way. The last thing she wanted to do was burn bridges that we would need to cross again. As I submitted to her leadership, I continued to learn from her and follow her lead while witnessing amazing results, which I implement to this day. So remember your assignment is to be a light and sponge supporting both your leader and staff.

"Serving and honoring those in leadership as well as remaining teachable and coachable have positioned me for success both in ministry and during my career. I would also suggest getting a mentor. Wise counsel is always good when making decisions and exploring different opportunities."

Brittany Morton - MBA

"Serving on purpose is something I had to learn to do quickly. With students knocking on my door, not only for career advisement, but also advice with personal issues, I had to realize that there was a bigger picture. Making myself fully available for students not only gave them hope, but gave me fulfillment."

Letariel Jordan - College Academic Advisor

Start At the Bottom and Serve Your Way Up

I am sure you are familiar with the coined phrase, "Start at the bottom and work your way up." Well, I challenge that age old adage by encouraging you to take a more humble, less aggressive approach by *starting at the bottom and serving your way up*. I am of the opinion that a successful transition into the corporate arena starts with an attitude of humility, gratefulness and gratitude. A willingness to make yourself available to do what it takes to show your availability and support at the lowest level is important. As a new employee, your posture should consistently be "how can I help?" "How can I serve?"

I heard a story of a group of new hires going through orientation on their first day at work, being introduced to the staff by HR. At the beginning of the tour, they met the copy room team. A gentleman walked in and dropped off some papers to be copied. He made the assumption that one of the new hires was a member of the copy team. The new hire was offended and had a bad attitude, after all she was not there to make copies; she had just graduated with a degree. Towards the end of the tour, they passed by the CEOs office only to learn that the gentleman that was asking to have the copies made was the CEO. Remember, you never know who you will meet, so never think more highly of yourself than you should. In no way am I suggesting that you come in with little or no ambition to aspire to grow with the company, but be prepared at all times to fulfill the "other duties as an assigned" part of your job description at any given time with the right attitude.

There were times that I would start a new job and was asked to handle the most menial tasks and I would always respond with a good attitude. Early in my career I was asked as the HR Manager, to cover the phones and even help with trash at times. Although that was not my "job," I realized in the absence of staff, it was about doing what was in the best interest of the company. Many missed opportunities happen when we are so busy looking to have a head seat at the table rather than just being grateful for a seat at the table. Learning to serve in the shadows and bloom where you are planted is important. There will be days and moments where you feel like, "I was not hired for this" or may even find yourself frustrated with both your job and manager. I have been there, but remaining humble and willing to learn the processes and systems through what seems like the grunt work develops great character and skill. Humility always wins. I also personally believe that you should not be so quick to take the credit for a project that goes extremely well. If you are not equally excited to take all the blame if it turns out terribly sour. I believe that will help keep you humble, grateful and whistling while you work.

"Be humble. So often we hear about new, young employees coming into the workforce with an unrealistic sense of entitlement. While it is great to be ambitious and see the sky as the limit, it is very important to understand process, position, and timing. Also, respect the invaluable lessons you learn with the experience that you gain through growth and time. Remember, success is not a destination but a journey!"

Tayna Frett - MSM, Senior Vice President Administration and Facilities at Non-Profit Washington, D.C.

Create A Strategy For Success

Success does not happen by accident. It must be intentional. I am sure that most successful people will tell you that they make a resolute effort daily to reach their goals and attain success. Success is also a process. It is all about making healthy choices along your professional journey that will ultimately position you at the next crossroad where another choice must be made. Many new professionals do not make intentional steps toward being successful on a job. Typically, you are just excited that you were hired and show up daily to do your job. But you have no real strategy on how to make yourself a valuable and indispensable asset or no real plan on how to position yourself to grow. This is not to be confused with promotion versus positioning. This type of positioning has everything to do with learning all you can about what your current job entails, so that you are prepared for career track advancement when a door opens. Like anything else, it starts with making a decision to maintain a positive attitude, remain committed to the journey and bloom where you are planted despite the challenges you will face. Do not allow challenges to frustrate you out of position or out of your positive disposition. Stay focused! You will inevitably encounter challenging bosses, conflicting co-workers and personal nuances, but you must determine to accept every experience and use it towards your professional growth. Do not allow yourself to be distracted. Remember you are there on purpose.

I have seen too many young professionals easily enticed by the dollar. They never take enough time to learn all they can about the job before they are ready to hop off to another more enticing opportunity. I remember hearing an old adage that says, "A rolling stone never gathers any moss." Simply put, you can't attain anything that sticks if you are constantly moving. I would advise new professionals to make a commitment to an organization for at minimum of two to three years before moving on to the next best opportunity. Remaining stable and consistent will add to your success in a number of ways which will allow you to focus on growing, learning and building a solid resume that shows stability.

Opportunities for expansion are to help you enhance your skills so that you are ready for promotion. However, be sensible enough to assess when new career opportunities are offered and determine whether it is the right opportunity and the right time. It is important to realize that each positive and productive decision made on your professional journey equals a "win" or a "success." Even the poor personal or professional choices that we make add value to the grand scheme of things. Life is about learning and growing. Therefore, your corporate journey will consist of both successes and failures and while we celebrate both, realizing it all helps to grow and prepare you professionally. I have learned that in order to experience consistent wins, you must develop a strategy for success. I personally believe that it starts by becoming the CEO of your role. Simply put, take ownership of your position and everything that impacts it.

Whenever I started working for a company, I immediately took ownership and declared myself the CEO of my position. I always identified the goals for the role, the resources needed to complete all tasks, and created a strategy for success. I reviewed my predecessor's failures and successes and used it as a benchmark for my future goals. I always took ownership over my assignments and held myself accountable for deliverables and outcomes, as well as held myself responsible for failures, by reviewing every decision determining what could have been done better the next time. My objective was not just meeting my personal bottom line or goals, but also tying them into the company's bottom line as well. Your performance goals, which are usually identified in your position description and discussed during one-on-one meetings with your supervisor, are also a part of that bottom line. I always created my own goals and developed my own core values and strategy for my piece of the organization.

It is important to know that while you should not enter an organization solely looking for the next promotional opportunity, you are certainly being hired by the organization with the possibility of you becoming a leader. Smart organizations and hiring managers are always looking into how they can hire assets and yield a return on investment even if not overnight. Wise hiring decisions are always made with future plans in mind. This is critical for new employees to keep in mind. You are being assessed daily for future growth and possible promotional opportunities. What you do or neglect to do will impact the decision makers when the time comes. Companies are always looking to hire what Jack Welch refers to as "A" players. These are employees who are the best at what they do regardless of the position you are hired for. You can have a receptionist or janitor who is an "A" player simply because they are not marginal or subpar, but rather reliable, dependable and committed to excellence. With that in mind, you should always strive to be an "A" player because you never know when that next opportunity might open up.

Most organizations require you to be in a position for 30-90 days before a request for transfer is honored. I have personally requested that management override that rule on a number of occasions and make an exception in order to promote someone who has been exceptional. Be exceptional. Another very important key to success is being solution driven. Remember you were chosen and hired because of the skills you possess as well as the potential you have to be a leader, which means you are expected to be solution-driven.

As a leader in training, you should be able to readily identify problems. No one wants to work with someone who is only problem prone or complaining about what's wrong, but never able to offer an answer. A true leader not only exposes the issues, but also proposes viable solutions. Chances are your leader is not oblivious to the issues around them that need to be resolved. They really commend and welcome the input of those who can identify suggestions and solutions. Being a problem solver always adds value to the bigger picture. So, as you attain opportunities recognize the need to create a solid strategy for success which should include proposing solutions. My personal experience when creating and implementing success strategies during my career has always resulted in promotion.

> *"I would advise new professionals not to be constant complainers. If you have an issue, discuss it with your supervisor and always be prepared to go in with a well thought out resolution."*

Donna Brooks - Retired Military
Support Operations Division, Logistics Specialist

> *"Often times, we want the perfect situation, perfect person to work for and with before we dish out any good work. The reality is that every environment just will not be perfect and that is ok! Look for ways to learn and be developed even if you are in an undesired environment. Remind yourself everyday why you are there and master the art of being productive no matter what! I kept the right perspective and it paid off!"*

Lauren A. Ward - MBA
Speech Language Pathologist

Positioning vs. Promotion

Pick a direction and grow! These are the words I would constantly hear from my SVP of Human Resources as he encouraged me to position myself beyond the four walls of my job. Reluctant at times because of my fear of networking as a new professional, I would avoid any opportunity to attend external meetings, networking functions or training classes. I was happy in my comfort zone, arriving to work on time every day and just doing my job, in hopes of doing a good enough job that I would be promoted from within. However, I quickly learned that the smaller the organization, the slimmer your chances for internal promotion. I realized that if I was going to advance in my career, I needed to take advantage of the encouragement my supervisor gave me to go. It is not often you have people who are truly invested in seeing you soar. If you are ever assigned to someone who takes an interest in you, be grateful and listen to their wisdom. After several nudges from my supervisor I started getting out there and connecting. I eventually became comfortable with and excited about my professional growth opportunities, which eventually opened doors for other career and business connections.

New professionals must seek to be positioned and not just promoted. When you look for positioning and not just promotion, promotion is inevitable. Look for growth opportunities through *It is important to understand that positioning is better than just promotion.* professional development sources, networking functions and professional organizations. I remember working at a company where I attended every lunch and learn, HR networking function, workshop and seminar. I also joined and facilitated every focus group, meeting, task force, committee, networking function and professional group, such as Toastmasters, that my Director encouraged me to participate in. It was all training ground that helped to groom me for my future. I met a number of amazing people networking that often led to my next opportunity. Remember, you are not on your job just to be promoted from within. But rather you are on assignment to do a job and be positioned for growth, character building and advancement for the next opportunity, which may or may not be within that particular organization.

Work towards the possibility of promotion, but do not be disappointed if it does not happen there. Instead, take what you learn daily and grow with it. Wise employees take advantage of every resource and opportunity at their disposal and endeavor to connect with like-minded peers, mentors and coaches. When you enter the corporate arena, it would be in your best interest to learn about all of the resources the company offers and figure out how you can use them to develop your skills and even learn new ones.

One of your top priorities should be to focus on developing yourself as a professional wherever you are. Often, professionals are looking for opportunity for advancement when they should be looking for opportunities for expansion. Advancement is great at the proper time, but until that opportunity presents itself, look to expand your knowledge and skills through resources like professional books and trainings, workshops, conferences and professional mentors to help you as you grow professionally. Identifying a mentor you can trust to help you make sound decisions along your journey is wise. Mentors help you see the big picture as you position yourself.

When you interview, you should always ask what opportunities the company offers to help you grow in your future role; not necessarily what promotional opportunities exist or whether they offer succession plans. Employers want to hire good people with vision and drive that can be harnessed and managed. Questions about promotional opportunities too soon are a turn off. When you start your career, you must take responsibility for your growth. Every opportunity may not be preparing you for internal promotion, but will certainly assist you with your overall career endeavors. Where you are now is only a part of the grand scheme of things.

As a HR professional, I have always encouraged my staff to seek opportunities to be positioned. I have always been a firm believer in promoting professional growth and always assisted my staff with whatever they wanted to accomplish, whether it was with my current company or when they were ready to move on.

I remember plenty of opportunities that I accepted or created with the bigger picture in mind. As mentioned, I offered to lead committees, to develop my meeting, facilitating and leadership skills, as well as joined Toastmasters to develop my presentation ability. Although I gained those skills some 10 years ago, I am still being positioned as a result of the fruit. Remember, it is all about positioning.

Let's Talk

Business communications is probably one of the most requested corporate training subjects today. With challenges like cultural and generational barriers, along with the warp speed advancement of technology, communicating for effectiveness has become quite a challenge. While teaching a college course on business communications 10 years ago, I discussed things like formatting letters and emails. Now we have a number of traditional as well as non-traditional tools for communication, to include everything from phone messaging apps to various social media platforms. Of course, the less preferred option is good ole face-to-face interaction. However, despite the method chosen, there are a few keys to successful business communication. First, I would always encourage you to seek to hear and not only be heard in any verbal or written communication. In addition, it is not only about what you say, but how you say it. It is very important to curb your thoughts to be sure they are professional in choice of words, as well as tone. You must develop the art of communicating with both diplomacy and tact.

Too often I have observed in-person as well as email communications that are easily misinterpreted because there was no audible voice behind them, which is why I prefer face to face conversations, opposed to hiding behind emails and other online communications. Too often to avoid confrontation or conflict, we hide behind emails and honestly it adds more confusion. I would always advise you to seek clarity in person. Whenever you are writing a letter, sending an email, communicating through business text message or any form of instant messaging, it is important to understand that the timing of a message delivery and tone are also important. Also, as difficult as it may be, sometimes you must remember to always remove your emotions from your communications, especially if the topic of discussion or conversation gets heated. The wisest thing to do is walk away and return to respond once you have gathered yourself. If need be, allow a neutral and unbiased person to review and curb your responses to be sure it is absent of emotion and sarcasm. It took me a long time to learn that lesson.

As an unseasoned professional, I was always ready to snap back, especially when communicating with condescending or unprofessional employees who attempted to aggravate me. You will have your fair share of challenges, but breathe, take a step back, walk away and think about your response. It is always the most professional way to handle any heated form of communication. I learned a number of tough lessons and would caution you that there are consequences for quick unfiltered responses. I would also advise you to avoid the habit of "reply all" to group emails, especially with emails that come across as finger pointing or accusatory. Always seek resolution face-to-face. As you grow professionally, this becomes easier. However, you would be surprised at the number of seasoned professionals who still fall prey to the communication pitfall because they choose to be ruled by their emotion and ego.

As a new professional, do not fall into this trap! Remember, it is all business and none of it is personal. Your responsibility is to diplomatically and tactfully communicate in a professional and respectful manner in all instances. Unfortunately, many managers and supervisors have not mastered the art of effective communication. Be patient with your leader, but remember that does not exempt employees from respectfully identifying ways to open up lines of engagement. Fostering healthy communication is critical for successful, professional relationships and corporate success.

Because there are a variety of ways to communicate, intent can get lost. It is helpful to always seek to clarify. Perception is just as important as intent. If the person receiving the communication is insulted, offended or perceives it as rude or condescending, even though that was not your intent, it is important to acknowledge how they feel and resolve the situation. The best way to accomplish this is face-to-face. Poor and misconstrued communication can damage professional relationships.

The Balancing Act

Commit to excellence rather than perfection and never ever over commit. It is important as a new professional that you develop balance early in your career. I remember having a colleague who complained constantly about being over worked and underpaid. She came in extra early and worked extra late. I often wondered if she was a poor manager of her time. What it boiled down to was she just wanted to go "above and beyond" with the hope of being recognized as a dedicated employee. That was great if that was her method for advancement. The only issue was she complained all of the time, especially when management would request that she be on special projects that required extra hours. She eventually started having trouble at home because of the long hours, which led to her neglecting her family.

Even without family commitments, the same holds true for new professionals. Do not over commit or neglect your other responsibilities, social connections and outlets trying to make a name for yourself or please a boss. It is easy to get out of balance quickly if we are not careful. Hard work is commendable, but you must develop professional boundaries early on. This is very important. It is tricky because as we know you should always strive to do your very best, especially at the start of your new opportunity considering there is usually a probationary period where your performance is evaluated. So while I am in support of you pushing yourself during your probationary period to learn all you can, I would recommend that you taper back a little, create some balance and develop your own pace once you have fully learned the job.

Once you have learned your job duties, I would suggest

only pushing yourself beyond your scope of responsibilities on a project by project basis. This may sound anti-work, but honestly it is not. I have watched many people crash and burn because they lacked balance. To avoid this imbalance, I would first advise against volunteering to take on much more than the responsibilities you were hired for until you are fully familiar with the job. However, if you are asked to assist with a project, you should do so if possible. Be sure to be honest about the amount of time you can commit in relation to other projects, responsibilities and deadlines. The section in the job description that says "other duties as assigned" means we are not exempt from random responsibilities and projects. However, you should not avail yourself to biting off more than you can chew too soon. It may be difficult to give a little pushback as a newbie since you are eager to please. However, it is wise to do so and not risk being overwhelmed which will eventually leave you unproductive and resentful.

The easiest way to manage your professional balance is to stay in constant communication with your supervisor about what is on your plate. I recall a number of times when I either sincerely wanted to help with projects I felt I could really make an impact on or I was assigned to something I had absolutely no interest in. You would think that in either instance my supervisor should have been able to see that I had a full plate considering the last three projects and the one I was currently working on came from them. The question is, when they choose not to see that your plate is full, how do you pushback and not seem like you do not want to be a team player? I would always start by sifting through the projects and determine what was directly related to my primary role and not get distracted. Ultimately, the easiest way to develop professional balance is not to overextend yourself too soon. Learn your role, observe and wait before accepting much more and stay in constant communication with the person giving the marching orders. On several occasions I had two directors literally pulling me in different directions which always resulted in competing priorities. You are responsible for your balance which includes communicating your concerns. Most organizations that promote work life balance mean well when they add additional work. Chances are, you have been identified as being good at what you do. However, it is ok to respectfully say "I can't." It will help you to avoid lots of stress.

Overachievers and dedicated professionals often set precedents that lead to expectations from their management and coworkers. Certain things do not need to be listed in your job description anymore. It is enough for them to assume that there are tasks that you should be doing based on how well you performed in prior times. It is very difficult to pull back after you have set such high expectations.

> *"As a young professional, I had to learn a balance between my personal and professional life. Often, I would take on more than I could handle. Therefore, I would advise young professionals to create clear goals and set boundaries for themselves and others. In doing this, one can avoid the pitfalls of burnout, fatigue, and other stress related sicknesses."*
>
> *Gentry Simmons - Masters in Executive Leadership Teacher, Speaker and Coach*

Do Not Fire Yourself: Play by the Rules

One of the simplest ways to secure your position in any organization is to adhere closely to company policy. After reviewing the company handbook and conducting orientation with new hires, I would make this statement, "We never fire employees; employees eliminate themselves." That statement was never meant to intimidate or discourage new hires. Whenever a decision was made to terminate an employee based on performance, I always made it clear that we have exhausted all measures before deciding to let anyone "go".

It is important for new professionals to exercise good stewardship by following company policies and procedures closely. I have been in HR for over 25 years and I can honestly say that I have had to part ways with a number of employees for a myriad of reasons. However, in all my years of working, I have never *fired* one person. I am a firm believer that I do not fire people; they fire themselves. While this may sound like a harsh statement, I have found that it is true. Because I am a professional that operates in integrity, I would never terminate someone without just cause. Before a decision is made to terminate an employee, unless it was for gross misconduct, it is the responsibility of the employer to do their due diligence by investigating the details of every situation and be sure that all the facts are sound and that all measures have been exhausted before termination is executed.

As a new employee you must understand that policies are in place for a reason. If the policy says, "No excessive telephone use, internet or social media use while at work," then that is exactly what is expected. You can be sure that anything connected to the company network to include company computers, cell phones, etc. are being monitored. Company property can be accessed without your approval at any time. To avoid problems, I would advise you to follow the rules. It always amazed me how employees who would totally break the rules, but get upset when reprimanded. It is also important to comply with rules even when you are not being monitored and regardless of whether you agree. In most states, a company that offers employment at-will can terminate for a good reason, bad reason or no reason at all so please follow rules to avoid losing your job over something trivial. It is also important to be careful not to get caught up or identified with employees who are defiant finger pointing rabble-rousers who often break rules and have their own agenda. Stay focused, intentional and professional at all times.

No Fair Play: Avoid Office Politics

Many new professionals are blind-sided by what is referred to as "office politics" simply because there are no rules for the game. Office politics are strategies and games people play in order to gain an advantage in the workplace. When you enter the corporate world, there are a number of things you need to be aware of to avoid this professional pitfall. The most important thing to remember is that you do not have friends in the workplace. At the end of the day, each person is either there for a paycheck, personal professional reward, opportunity for personal advancement or all of the above. It is not often that you find anyone looking to help you advance forward without seeking to gain something in return. And while you might want to give people the benefit of doubt, I would still caution you to be wise in your conversations. In the rare case that you do come across someone positioned to assist you in your career advancement, be grateful, but still keep your eyes open. Avoid water cooler conversations, gripe sessions or putting trust in co-workers with personal or confidential information. The term "dog eat dog" comes to mind when I think about some of the situations I encountered early in my career innocently getting caught in crossfire or manipulated to engage in conversations and agendas for personal gain.

The most difficult part of navigating office politics is that there is no playbook! You either learn from experience or someone. I remember working at an organization early on in my career where people were always negative and complaining about everything; being cut throat, fighting to get to the top and I always found myself amongst these people because they were very crafty at getting co-workers to rally around their frustrations or concerns and stir up discontent amongst the staff. Beware of those people. Often with office politics, it is all about manipulation and personal agenda.

If you go into an organization with pure motives and the intent to operate as a professional, you will be fine. If you keep observing, you will quickly be able to discern who is who. Keep your hands and your name clean.

Leave A Professional Legacy

Have you ever met or worked with someone whose absence was immediately felt when they left? Whether it is their kind smile, warmth in conversation or dedicated work ethic, you can immediately feel when they are no longer around. This should be your goal when you are preparing to move on in your career. Your time at the organization should have been so impressionable that you and the value you have added are sincerely missed. Too often new professionals come into an organization completely satisfied with getting a paycheck and going home. They have no interest in making a lasting impression.

Many new professionals never really take the time to learn and perform in their role with excellence or determine how they can be used to touch the lives of those around them both personally and professionally. You must become a master at your role and not just coast in order to leave a legacy. Employees should always strive to give their position their all. Do not be a slacker. Aspire to be known for submitting quality work that is always presented with excellence before deadlines.

Equally important is your responsibility to figure out how you can enhance your role to benefit the organization at-large. Look for ways to save money in the budget or streamline process. Many young professionals fail to realize, what you put in professionally, is what you will get out professionally. Make sure that your work ethic, dedication to the job and your availability is so outstanding that you leave your successor not only an easy and successful transition into the role, but you also leave them some big shoes to fill. When you are ready to move on, you should leave such an impact that your absence is truly felt. Also develop such a strong professional image and brand for yourself that staff name you when they are looking to reference someone who worked with professionalism, integrity and excellence. I will be the first to admit that you will certainly be challenged along the way, but it is a part of the journey and I trust that you will be fine.

I received a call from one of my previous Directors who was having a serious marital problem. I was shocked she thought to call me years after I had left the company. However,

I remember the days I would go into her office and pray with her about a number of personal and professional situations. I suppose her comfort level, prompted her to call me at one of the most devastating times in her life. Leaving a legacy is more than just the work you do on the job, but it is also about who you impact along the way.

"Be determined to give your highest and best to your position and do not get discouraged when faced with challenges. Learn to manage your time wisely so you are able to successfully meet goals and deadlines."

Teresa Brown – BBA
Director of Administration

Depart In Peace

It is just as important for a new professional to transition into the corporate arena successfully as it is to transition from one opportunity to another gracefully. You must remember that your first opportunity is just the beginning of your career and it is important to develop a healthy track record of leaving with integrity, which includes everything from your volunteer opportunities, to your internship, to your first paid position. It must all be handled professionally. Never burn bridges by leaving without notice. This is all a part of leaving a professional legacy. Once I helped a man get a job that he literally pleaded for. He hit the ground running and did an awesome job. Later I found out that less than six months later a more lucrative opportunity was offered and he accepted the job, but he gave no notice to his current employer which made him "non-re-hirable." If he would have given notice he could have added the job on his resume with no problems and been eligible for re-hire if he ever needed to return. It is very important to exit jobs with integrity, never leaving an employer high and dry. I would also caution you on the integrity of a company who will not allow you the courtesy of putting in a two week notice with your current employer. What it all boils down to is, a true professional understands the importance of being a good steward over every opportunity from inception to completion. You never know what opportunity is ahead and who you will need as a reference or connection. I will always encourage every professional to depart in peace.

Chapter 4

Discover You
The Entrepreneur

There are lots of bad reasons to start a company. But there is only one good,
legitimate reason: it's to change the world."
Phil Libin- CEO of Evernote

Not everyone desires to be an entrepreneur. It takes a specific personality to embrace the responsibilities, discipline, diligence and tenacity needed to start and run a successful business. It is about more than having a great idea. It is also about having a vision for how to build, grow and brand the idea. I am sure any successful entrepreneur would agree that it is hard work.

Many young innovative and forward thinking graduates are leaning towards being their own boss. Many young professionals desire to do something more meaningful than your typical 9 to 5. Many are seeing the world and opportunities through a different lens and making the decision to take the leap of faith in starting their own businesses. My favorite entrepreneur, Christina Brown, who is founder of Love Brown Sugar, shares her story on how she started her career in the corporate world and eventually made the decision to take the leap of faith and build her own brand which is going on 6 years strong. She does not claim to be an expert, but I am sure you would agree, she is quite the entrepreneur-realist. Check out her interview below:

MM: What is your personal definition of an entrepreneur?

LBS: An entrepreneur is somebody who is not afraid to take risks and values the importance of ownership and self-employment. It does not necessarily have to be somebody who quits their job on a whim. A true entrepreneur takes calculated risks with the understanding that your highest paying gig isn't the one that pays you the most money, but the one that allows you to live a comfortable life with passion and purpose.

MM: Please tell me when and how you knew you were supposed to be working for yourself.

LBS: When I was sitting at my day job and I said to myself "I can do this - for myself." I transitioned from working in a corporate environment when my job and my side-hustle began to battle each other for my time. I started getting calls from potential clients, having to spend way more time on my side-hustle because it was actually paying me well and I started unfortunately, neglecting and resenting my office work. That's when I knew it was time to make a decision. Either I needed to quit my side hustle completely or it was time to take it more seriously. I chose the latter.

MM: Please share the major differences between working for yourself and working for someone else.

LBS: People assume working for yourself is this glamorous lifestyle where you sit around in your PJ's all day indulging in ice cream and reality TV, go on trips whenever you want and for however long you want, while simultaneously paying your bills. NO SUCH THING. I work harder now as an entrepreneur than I ever did in corporate. Entrepreneurship is grueling, tiresome and most times - unglamorous. Because this is MY business, there's a higher level of ownership and accountability and so I end up working late nights and early mornings, weekends and every bit of time in between to make my dreams a reality.

MM: Please share your greatest challenge at the start of your entrepreneurship and how did you overcome it.

LBS: My greatest challenge and something I actually am still working on daily is developing discipline. Being in a corporate or full-time setting, there are certain day to day regulations and expectations that are filtered down from your job. You have a set time you need to be in the office, and generally a set time when it is acceptable to leave. You have certain protocol like a "lunch hour" and also deadlines that are passed down to you by your managers. When you choose a life of business ownership, you are now your own manager. So a lot of those processes that you learned in the corporate world still apply, but now you have to enforce them on yourself. That means getting up and showing up on time, adhering to deadlines you set for yourself and being accountable (to your clients, to your staff and also to yourself).

MM: What makes you successful today?

LBS: I am not afraid to fail. Something that holds so many entrepreneurs back is the fear of failure. You take your time opening up your business or push back deadlines you set for yourself because you are worried about something going wrong. Newsflash: Whatever can go wrong WILL go wrong, whether you plan for 10 years or plan for 10 minutes. It is inevitable that things will happen that are not according to plan. It will be frustrating. You might cry, or throw a few things against the wall. You might need therapy after. But you will live. And you will have 10x more successes than failures if you keep trying and let go of your fear.

MM: What barometer should one use to determine if entrepreneurship is for them?

LBS: Would you do this if no one paid you? Can you do this better than most other people? If you answered yes to both of those questions, then you might be ready to own a business of your own. Entrepreneurship is tough. Especially if you do not have your revenue stream figured out immediately. You literally have to have so much passion, that if what you are doing did not bring you money immediately, you would be ok with it. What should drive you is what you are doing, not the amount of money you are making from it. That's how you will, organically, become rich and successful. It should be something you are awesome at and have a passion for. If it is just one or the other, it is a recipe for failure (financially and emotionally).

MM: What type of mindset is critical for success as an entrepreneur?

LBS: The "I will not lose" mindset. You have to be very resilient as an entrepreneur. There are a lot of ups and downs. Some entrepreneurs fail miserably at one business and then go on to create multi-billion dollar companies years later. Successful entrepreneurs constantly innovate and they do not give up.

MM: What obstacles can you expect to face as an entrepreneur and how can you overcome them?

LBS: The obstacles are endless. People will have passion for working for and with you and then suddenly lose it and quit. Clients/customers will promise to pay and go back on their agreements with you. Sometimes you will be lonely (isolation is necessary for focus sometimes). There are so many. The way to overcome them is to identify what you do not like and take action. The only way to change something is to take action; less talking and more doing.

MM: What resources can assist with being successful?

LBS: A great team is priceless. The quicker you can identify your weaknesses, the faster you will be able to assemble a team of people who can help you fill in the gaps. As for me - I'm not that great at organizing. I have a bit of an organized chaos thing going on in my inbox, my office, and my overall life. I understand it, but most others do not. My first order of business was finding someone who could help me with overall organization and administration. Develop a team to help in those areas you lack. Other resources - a great calendar tool and also something that helps with time management. I'm partial to the Teux Deux app. It keeps my to-do lists in one place and it syncs with my devices so I can make changes anywhere and at any time.

MM: What is a brand and how do you develop a brand?

LBS: A brand is something iconic. It is something that is quickly and easily associated with a specific product, service or activity. Developing a brand is a tall order, but it starts with having a plan, being consistent and having tailored communication to the outside world about what you offer and what you stand for.

MM: Why is developing your brand important?

LBS: Your brand is everything. It is your reputation. It is your ticket to financial success, and it is also one thing no one else can take away from you (unless you let them).

MM: Can you briefly describe, in addition to your already mentioned answers, 3 keys to being a successful new entrepreneur?

LBS: 1. Do not be afraid to fail. Failure is inevitable. As long as you do not dwell on it, the failure makes you a better entrepreneur and grows you in ways that will dictate your future success. 2. Make discipline a daily practice. Entrepreneurship requires hard work and determination. If you do not have discipline, none of this will matter. 3. Make sure your vision and dreams connect seamlessly with your actions. Dreams and goals are great, but they're nothing without action. Do not just say it; do it.

Christina Brown is the founder of LoveBrownsugar.com, Babybrownsugar.com and Browngirlslove.com.

Follow @lovechristinabrown for more information on entrepreneurship and empowerment.

SO What's YOUR Excuse?

On April 26, 2012, 10 days after having my son, I was rushed to the hospital because of a headache. I had an aneurysm and there was blood on my brain. I had to have emergency brain surgery and doctors were afraid I would die. They said if I lived, I would not be able to see, talk or walk. I had to learn to walk, talk and see again. Today I am healed and well! Thank God HE had the final say over my life. I want to encourage you. If I can push past brain surgery; have another baby; start a ministry and write a book, certainly you can motivate yourself to pursue that business or career and be successful! With the basic information shared in this practical guide you should be ready to successfully start your career transition! It will be somewhat intimidating at first, but this guide should help you jump-start your process. Remember you are qualified for this next step in your professional journey. You have been prepared for this very moment. Take a deep breath; prepare and pursue! I am praying that you realize your optimal potential.

Words Of Wisdom (W.O.W)
Entering the Real World Workplace

I do not think there is anything more credible than hearing the professional advice given in this book echoed through the words of wisdom from a few of my preferred professionals, both young and seasoned.

Tayna Frett - MSM & SVP Administration & Facilities at Non-Profit in Washington DC

I started working (for money) at the age of 16. Prior to that I worked, during the summers, at my high school helping out with administrative tasks in the bookstore and finance office, providing help with any miscellaneous administrative tasks as requested. I officially started in the administrative field at the age of 16 and that's all I have been doing since. Early in my career I was definitely trying to find the balance between staying to myself, keeping my head down, just doing my job and learning the importance of building corporate relationships and establishing rapport. If I could offer any advice to new professionals, it would be to stay out of office politics and be very careful about that fine line between mixing business and personal. It is also important to understand who the players are, who's in charge; seek to collaborate, and more than anything, make sure that people know who you are, what you do, and the value that you bring to an organization.

Gentry Simmons - Masters in Executive Leadership
Teacher, Speaker and Coach.

I began working in my teens, but I entered my career as a teacher in my twenties. I have been in my career for ten years. During my tenure as a teacher, I taught English in various capacities at grade levels 6-12 and eventually college. I was fortunate to have a lot of guidance and mentorship when beginning my career. As a young professional, I still made mistakes. I had to learn a balance between my personal and professional life. Often, I would take on more than I could handle. Therefore, I would advise young professionals to create clear goals, and set boundaries for themselves and others. In doing this, one can avoid the pitfalls of burnout, fatigue, and other stress related sicknesses.

Willie F. Diggs II - LBSW, MSW
Assistant Professor
Department of Social Work, Counseling, and Psychology

I started working at the age of 16 and have been in the business of client services for over 20 years with 12 years of social work experience.

One of my first mistakes as a young professional was not taking advantage of the wisdom and guidance offered by senior leaders. It is very important that you soak up the knowledge of the individuals who are experts in your field. You should also learn the difference between constructive feedback and criticism. Early in my career I perceived every correction given as negative criticism, but as I have grown professionally, I later realized that most, if not all, corrections were good feedback and once applied, helped me to function at my highest potential. Another mistake I made early in my career was failing to develop a strategic plan for self-care. As a social worker you deal with vulnerable populations, and clients with various needs, so it is very easy to forget about the importance of taking care of yourself to include things like taking days off, making regular doctor visits, and developing a simple mental routine to make sure that you do not take on the issues of your clients.

I would encourage any new professional to enjoy the journey and have celebrations along the way. Become the expert in your field and do not sell yourself short because an agency or organization can't afford you; value apprenticeships and internships. They are the gateway into your next position and salary growth. Finally, treat everyone within your organization with respect. You never know who is going to provide you with access to your next position. Chances are it is not who you think. So, if you treat everyone with respect and dignity your seeds of friendliness will be received back to you.

Leonard Lawrence Curry Jr. - BS

I am currently a Computer Technician Logistics Lead II for a Microsoft Data Center. I started working when I was 15. I had a part time job at a gym as a facilities attendant while in high school. I have been in my career field for 2 years so far. One year as an Easy Tech at Staples and one year as a Computer Technician I.

I should have accepted more assistance from my parents or the available money from the government such as grants and scholarships so I would not have to worry about debt later.

I would advise any young professional to focus on something very broad in the beginning and then narrow down your focus on what you like about that broad topic once you have gained a little experience. I majored in computer science, but I worked in the warehouse for different retailers. Combining the two, I found it very easy to be the lead for one of the logistics departments at a Microsoft Data Center.

Brittany Morton - MBA

I started working on my 16th birthday! I have been working professionally for over 5 years. As a young professional, I thought that all I needed to land my dream job was a good GPA and a college degree. I quickly learned once I graduated from college, that there was so much more to be considered when preparing for success in the professional arena.

Do not be afraid to try new things, go new places and connect with new people. While in college, I stayed in my comfort zone. I did not take advantage of internships, study abroad or co-op opportunities and as I result, I wasn't as competitive in the job market. I have learned that the more exposure you get, the better off you will be. I would also suggest getting a mentor. Wise counsel is always good when making decisions and exploring different opportunities. Finally, remain flexible! Plans do not often go as planned, but if you keep the right mentality, remain teachable and humble, and are able to make the best out any situation, there is absolutely nothing that can stop you.

Danelle McClellan - BS, JD
Paralegal

I started working full time at the age of 24 and have been 13 years in the field. My greatest mistake in my professional career was underestimating my worth. I failed to adequately research salaries and positions and as a result, I was underpaid *and overworked for an extended amount of time. Explore your options. Never limit your professional goals based solely upon your degree(s) or areas of study. Take advantage of career counselors and life coaches that have the talent and ability to cultivate your passion into a purposeful career.*

Donna L. Brooks - Retired Military
Support Operations Division
Logistics Specialist

I started working in the summer job program sponsored by the city, at the age of fourteen. I joined the military at the age of 19. It was my first real job and I have been working as a logistician for the past 35 years.

If I could advise young professionals of anything it would be always pray before entering into the workplace, listen three times as much as you speak and be observant. Never turn down a training opportunity. Never enter a meeting without pen and paper. Do not be a constant complainer and if you have an issue/problem, discuss it with you supervisor, be prepared to go in with a resolution.

Teresa M. Brown - Bachelors in Business Administration
Director of Administration

I started working at age 15 and have been working in my career field for 30+ years. One major mistake I made as a young professional was accepting salaries that were offered to me without researching the positions and negotiating for what I was really worth. I was intimidated by others who "pretended" to be smarter than me. I would advise you to know your own strengths and do not expect others to point them out for you.

I would advise any young adult just starting out their career to determine to give your highest and best to your position and do not get discouraged when faced with challenges. Also, identify a mentor who you respect and trust. Also, learn to manage your time so that you do not get overwhelmed with responsibilities and are able to meet deadlines. Finally, maintain your ethics and integrity.

La Tonia Rush - Certified Life Coach and CEO of "A Conversation from the Heart"

I started working at the age of 8. My first job was at the cleaners that my aunt worked at in Ohio. She would take me to work with her and I would put the tags on the clothes as the customers brought them in. This was my first exposure to customer service. When I turned 16, I worked at McDonald's and then I started my career as an administrative assistant. I was in my 20's when I realized that this is what I wanted to do as a career. I have been in this field for 20 plus years and I am also a certified Life Coach.

I made several major mistakes as a young professional because I just did not know. I did not take a class or go to college. Actually, I dropped out of high school and later got my GED. One of the biggest challenges that I had to learn while working in the administration field was I lacked structure. I worked the early part of my career off of pure zeal. I enjoyed what I did and what I was learning, but did not really have training in how to properly assist people.

Later in life, I learned not to take things personally and how not to get offended so easily. I was always the first person that got the blame for things that did not turn out properly. I had to learn to let my "work" speak for me and not get upset when tension fell into the workplace. If I did everything I was asked to do and had back up to prove it, I was in a good place to defend myself respectfully.

I would advise any young professional just starting out in their career to not choose a career just for money. One of the ways you can feel fulfilled is to do what you love. Once you have identified the thing that you enjoy doing, get as much training for it as possible. Do not EVER stop learning. I would also suggest you find a career mentor to push and guide you. This should be a person that is either doing or have done what you would like to do as a career goal. This person should give you insight on what you may encounter and also encourage you to keep moving forward.

Lauren A. Ward MBA
Speech Language Pathologist

At 25 years old, I completed my Masters and began working as a Speech Language Pathologist. I have been working for just under 2 years for EBS Healthcare and 5 months as a private practice therapist.

When I finished graduate school and started a 9 month fellowship that is required of all new therapists, I was assigned the most challenging fellowship supervisor in this area. There were people who had left the county waiting for this particular therapist to retire before they returned. I could not believe that I was assigned to begin my career under her tutelage. She was tough, quite abrasive and relentless in her demands. She did not explain how to do things and made it impossible to learn any of the systems of my workplace. I remember dreading her monthly visits and thinking that she would tear me to shreds as rumors about her had suggested. Although she was in fact all of the things that I mentioned above; she was also brilliant in the speech setting and was an extremely great resource for me throughout that 9 month period. She was even a great reference to help me land the position at the private practice where I currently work.

I will be the first to admit that it is quite easy to get distracted by personalities and preferences that you miss the most important thing, the work that you are there to do. Often times, we want the perfect situation, perfect person to work for and with before we dish out any good work. The reality is that every environment just will not be perfect and that's ok. Many new hires are not on the track to promotions, raises and references because they are not able to move beyond the fact that work does not always feel as comfy as home. A great majority of the time it will not. Our perspective has to be on completing the job that needs to be done and being determined to be developed even if it is not comfortable, especially as a new hire. It is important to value development despite disappointment.

New professionals have high expectations when leaving the classroom and rightfully so. You have worked hard, you have accomplished and completed a great milestone and you want to be treated and paid well. Naturally, you unknowingly assume that you will land the perfect job making an unbelievable amount of money and that everyone will be helpful and courteous as you make the transition to your new position. But that may not happen. It is possible to end up with a really poor leader as a boss, or working for a company with systems and policies that obviously do not work well. Unlike college, you will not be able to simply switch professors, change your schedule or take it next semester. Learn to grow in an unfavorable place and not despise any amount of experience. There are many things that you can learn where you are if you can manage to stay focused. If I had thrown in the towel with my impossible supervisor, I would have missed the knowledge that I was able to glean from her. Had I allowed her personality to hide what she carried that could benefit me, I probably would not have made the strides that I have made in my career in just two years. I kept the right perspective and it paid off! Look for ways to learn and be developed even if you are in an undesired environment. Remind yourself everyday why you are there and master the art of being productive no matter what.

Jessica Baldwin - Social Worker
Department of Human Resources

I started working at 15 years old. The mistake I made as a young professional was thinking I could do everything on my own. I bought into this way of thinking because others also thought I was capable and did not need help. I would highly advise any young professional to learn the policies of your company. It is very important to know the laws, expectations and regulations your organization operate under. Many companies will only support you when you operate within organizational guidelines. I would also advise any new professional to learn the art of self-care and do not work harder for someone else than you are willing to work for yourself. Balance is the key!

Contact Information

Rashida Selise Wilson

selisespeakslife@yahoo.com

www.selisespeakslife.com

Made in the USA
Lexington, KY
19 August 2017